The main focus of the book concentrates upon the sixty-four officers of the British Army's 19th Division (including a small number who were attached from elsewhere) who were either killed or died of wounds during the storming of the heavily-fortified village of La Boisselle, on the Somme, during early July 1916. The initial chapters deal with events from autumn 1914, when the area was captured from the French by the advancing Germans, through the deployment of British regiments the following year, the localised trench raids and digging of mine shafts, and the events of 1 July 1916, when the British attack was totally thwarted after sustaining heavy casualties. A separate section explores the reasons why certain individuals felt compelled to become officers in the first place, often dictated by their pre-war social standing, or simply because the authorities felt they possessed the necessary military attributes to do so. The later chapters deal with the region until the Armistice and beyond, plus a detailed breakdown of casualty figures for all ranks. Apart from a small number of books giving a general background to the village's capitulation, there has not been an in-depth volume dedicated solely to the endeavours of the 19th Division. (Whilst the officers provide the structure for the narrative, the bravery and contribution of the men who followed them into battle is not overlooked. One of them was awarded a Victoria Cross, as was his overall Commanding Officer, plus a gallant lieutenant who fell in action, and all three are indicative of the chaos and courage of the close-quarter fighting experienced by private soldiers through to lieutenant colonels alike). Contained within this text are eye-witness accounts (including some recently uncovered), war diary entries, numerous photographs of the fallen (a small proportion of these involved a lengthy search to obtain, and the collection as a whole has never been collated in one place before), biographical details, contemporary and modern images (a handful of the former have rarely been given a public platform), and a critical overview of the battle as it unfolded. Coming so soon after the well-documented slaughter of 1 July 1916, the hard-fought tactical success at La Boisselle – resulting in 3,500 casualties, of which 1,000 lost their lives – is sometimes overlooked within the wider history of the Great War.

Born in 1967, Nick Thornicroft grew up near Stroud in Gloucestershire, attending local schools before embarking upon a career in the funeral trade in 1985. He developed an abiding interest in local, national and world history from an early age, and his main focus lies within a long-standing fascination for the First World War. He has written and self-published two books on local war memorials, including Amberley, Box and Woodchester (one volume), and Bisley, Eastcombe and Oakridge (another single volume). He has also written a similar volume detailing the war dead of the three north Cornish villages of Tintagel, Boscastle and St. Gennys. In addition, The History Press has published two books: *Gloucestershire and North Bristol: Soldiers on the Somme*, and *Cornwall's Fallen: The Road to the Somme*, both of which focus upon servicemen from these respective counties who lost their lives at the Somme on 1 July 1916. Another self-published book was *The VCs of Gloucestershire and North Bristol*, detailing each recipient from the county who has been awarded the Victoria Cross since its inception in 1856. Nick has always sought to uncover the faces and voices of individuals in battle, believing this is one of the most powerful ways in which to even begin to comprehend the gallantry and sacrifice displayed by ordinary men in the heat of combat.

Dauntless Courage on the Somme

Officers of the 19th Division Who Fell at La Boisselle
1–10 July 1916

Nick Thornicroft

To Chris
Best wishes
Nick

AUGUST 2016

Helion & Company Limited

Helion & Company Limited
26 Willow Road
Solihull
West Midlands
B91 1UE
England
Tel. 0121 705 3393
Fax 0121 711 4075
Email: info@helion.co.uk
Website: www.helion.co.uk
Twitter: @helionbooks
Visit our blog http://blog.helion.co.uk/

Published by Helion & Company 2016
Designed and typeset by Mach 3 Solutions Ltd (www.mach3solutions.co.uk)
Printed by Short Run Press, Exeter, Devon

Text © Nick Thornicroft 2016
Images © as individually credited
Maps drawn by George Anderson © Helion & Company 2016

Front cover: Drawing titled 'The British offensive in France: the struggle for the conquest of La Boisselle', originally published in the Italian magazine *La Domenica del Corriere* on 16 July 1916. Rear cover: An aerial view of the Lochnagar Crater and the south-western tip of La Boisselle. The Glory Hole is situated on the rough ground between the houses and the open fields to the left. The 19th Division attacked the village from both sides (advancing from left to right). Mash Valley lies beyond the houses furthest from the camera. (Photograph courtesy of Jeremy Banning: <www.jeremybanning.co.uk>)

ISBN: 978-1-910777-82-4

British Library Cataloguing-in-Publication Data.
A catalogue record for this book is available from the British Library.

For details of other military history titles published by Helion & Company Limited contact the above address, or visit our website: http://www.helion.co.uk.

We always welcome receiving book proposals from prospective authors.

Contents

List of Illustrations and Maps

Preface

During the course of research for other books and articles, the place name 'La Boisselle' kept cropping up again and again. It was not, perhaps, surprising, in that two of the battalions which formed part of the 19th Division – 8th Gloucestershire Regiment (henceforth abbreviated to 8/Glosters) and 10/Worcesters – contained within their ranks a significant proportion of men from Gloucestershire, the county where I grew up. For example, the small hamlet of Amberley, near Stroud, lost three of its sons[1] as a direct result of the fighting at La Boisselle on 3 July, 1916.

On gravestones, church memorials and within newspaper reports of the battle, 'La Boisselle' seemed a constant marker within the wider war, almost demanding to grab my attention. It certainly succeeded. I have visited the village on a number of occasions, walked the battlefield, stood on the edge of the immense Lochnagar Crater – blown at 7:28 am on 1 July 1916 to destroy a German redoubt – and paused at the local cemeteries.

La Boisselle itself lay on the axis of the British offensive on the Somme, but by the end of that fateful day at the beginning of July 1916, the village was still in German hands, ferociously and expertly defended by a tenacious enemy. Within hours, as the dead still lay in no man's land and the wounded blocked the communication trenches, the 19th Division was brought up from its reserve position in preparation for a renewed attack. What had started at daybreak with great optimism for a decisive breakthrough had ended at twilight in unimaginable carnage, and for the men tasked with attempting to breach the same defences, the physical evidence which presented itself as they moved closer towards the firing line must have taxed even the most experienced veterans. It was made all the more remarkable because each and every one of the soldiers in the ranks was a volunteer, and the majority of the junior officers who led them had only been in such a role of authority for less than two years.

The Battle of the Somme as a whole became a series of short, localised and invariably bloody encounters as French, British and Empire troops tried to seize control

---

1   Three men of 8/Glosters – L/Cpl Wallace Marsh, Private Frederick Click & Private Leonard Melsome – all perished at La Boisselle between 3–7 July (Melsome was a stretcher bearer assisting the wounded in no man's land when he was shot in the head and later succumbed to his wounds).

Figure 1.1 The Cross of the 19th Division Memorial, opposite La Boisselle church. By the evening of 3 July, 1916, men of the division had breached the German front line, and were holding a position close by, ready to renew their attack in the morning. (Author's collection)

of German-held villages, ridges and copses, all fortified in depth with machine-gun nests, barbed wire entanglements, deep dugouts and intricate support lines which snaked back many miles.

To write a book about *every* soldier who fell during a particular Somme engagement would require a hefty volume each time, so I have focused upon the officers – from second lieutenant to lieutenant colonel – who carried out the brigade and staff orders without question, often advanced at the head of their men, faced a hail of bullets and bombs, and fell for the cause which was still almost unanimously popular, even at this halfway stage of a war which had already consumed many lives.

It is not intended to be a re-evaluation of the capture of La Boisselle, nor does it reveal new and insightful evidence as to how the ground was secured. It simply records how a group of men, thrown together by fate and army orders, stormed a seemingly impregnable village in Picardy, and, by doing so, provide historians an opportunity to commend their supreme achievement and dauntless courage which continues to defy the odds even to this day.

Acknowledgements

In my quest to uncover photographs of the fallen officers, I contacted numerous universities, colleges, schools, regimental museums, organisations and newspapers, and therefore many of the images, plus some of the personal information contained within this book, are as a result of the endeavours of individual archivists at a variety of different establishments. I have (hopefully) included all of the relevant acknowledgements and gratitude due within the officers' stories themselves, and my sincere apologies go to anyone inadvertently omitted. I thank everyone who has helped and contributed in this way, and just by way of a cautionary note relating to copyright, the rights of certain images reprinted here do not belong to the author, but to the person or place stated beneath each photograph. I have also tried to locate (to the best of my knowledge) the owners of copyrighted material, and labelled them as such, although there may be some omissions or errors which are genuinely unforeseen. (It is also worth noting that some of the images were sourced from original newspapers of the time, and do not reproduce well, even with the benefit of modern technology).

Amongst the individuals who made this book possible in other ways, I am greatly indebted to Malcolm Marjoram, a diligent and hard-working researcher who pored over countless newspaper archives on my behalf, as well as pursuing documents at the National Archives in Kew when I was unable to make the journey due to other commitments. His contribution to this book was immeasurable.

Pam and Ken Linge have embarked upon a gargantuan task of finding as many photographs as possible of the 72,000 + servicemen whose names are inscribed on the Thiepval Memorial to the Missing of the Somme. They very kindly took the time to compare 'their' list with 'mine', and we swapped images of those neither of us had in our collections before. I commend their project, and their enthusiasm to help.

I would also like to thank Bob Richards for providing information on Cornish links to some of the officers; Josie Brown for her sketch of 'Mash Valley' and La Boisselle; the Imperial War Museum for their guidance; The Naval & Military Press Ltd for their advice on the use of quotes from *Some Letters From A Subaltern On The Western Front*, and permission to use other images; 'Tommies Guides' (Menin House) for permission to use quotes from *Lander's War*; the staff at the National Archives, Kew; Gloucestershire Archives; Jeremy Banning; Wycliffe College, Stonehouse; the Dorset Regiment Museum; the editors of all the newspapers who granted permission to use photographs and extracts from their archives (a full list is to be found at the end of this book); Heather Edwards-Hedley (Haileybury School); Grace Pritchard-Woods (Cornwall Record Office); Charles Knighton (Clifton College, Bristol); Zoe Parsons (Kingswood School, Bath); Caroline Mannion (Cheshire Regiment Museum); Caru James (Llanelli Library); Malcolm Sloan (Cheltenham College); Jane Pendry & Terry Rogers (Marlborough College); Barbara Gent (Giggleswick School); Pat Davitt (Monmouth School); Caroline Benson (Reading University); Dr. Robin Darwall-Smith (The Master and Fellows of University College, Oxford); James Friendship (Plymouth College); Keith Haines (Campbell College, Belfast); Derek Bartley (Wales Search); Jeff Elson (Staffordshire Regiment Museum); Richard Meunier (Barts Health NHS Trust); Jane Jones (WW1 Photos); Murray Guest (Armidale School, Australia); Angela Tarnowski (Sherwood Foresters Museum); Andy Teal; Elen Simpson (Bangor University); Sarah Maxted & Lesley Koulouris (Berkhamsted School); Julian Reid (Corpus Christi College, Oxford); Liz Larby (Gresham's School, Norfolk); Emma Goodrum (Worcester College, Oxford); Alison Wheatley (King Edward VI School, Birmingham); Alan Curragh; Royal Belfast Academical Institution archives; Celia Green (Regimental Museum of the Royal Welsh) and my family, who indulge my passion for the First World War and actively encourage its development.

I am also greatly indebted to Duncan Rogers and Dr Michael LoCicero of Helion & Company Ltd, who provided much needed enthusiasm, practical guidance and positive encouragement to see this book through from its raw beginnings to a viable undertaking.

All historians and writers of historical conflict are mindful that the portrayal of death in battle is, of course, an emotive subject, and one which should be treated with

Figure 2.1 Contemporary postcard depicting captured trenches at La Boisselle.
(Author's Collection)

compassion. Some years ago I recall contacting the brother of two Second World War casualties, in the hope he would provide assistance in compiling information about his siblings, only to be told in no uncertain terms: "Leave the past where it is". I was somewhat taken aback, but this was *his* grief and *his* way of coping – who was I to say which was the right or wrong attitude to take?

My great-grandfather's brother, Private George Thomas Thornicroft, 1/Royal Warwickshire Regiment, lost his life in Flanders on 23 October, 1914. For many years, his portrait hung on a wall in the family home, but no one ever mentioned 'Uncle George'. He once lived there, he went to war, he never returned. Should we still feel the need to commemorate all our 'Uncle George's' today? One consequence of dying for freedom is that everyone who follows is entitled to their own point of view, so we acknowledge those who remember, as well as those who choose to forget. We have been given that choice, and this book represents mine.

Introduction

The 19th (Western) Division came into existence during September 1914, just one month after war had been declared. As tens of thousands of new recruits answered Lord Kitchener's[1] call to arms, they were allocated to the recently formed 'New Armies'. A logistical problem was soon encountered, however, as the number of experienced officers and non-commissioned officers (chiefly corporals and sergeants) available to train the eager volunteers into a viable military unit was woefully inadequate. Despite the hurried recall of those on reserve, retired, or overseas, the question needed to be addressed immediately, leading to the appointment of individuals often with little or no military training – other than their involvement within an Officer Training Corps at their former school or college – as soon-to-be leaders of men on the battlefield. It is entirely down to the sterling character of this 'civilian army', of all ranks, that the former solicitors, dock-workers, miners and bankers turned themselves into an efficient fighting force which was able to match, and eventually overcome, a considerable foe.

A pre-war officer cadet took an entirely structured route to becoming a significant rank in his chosen career, with attendance at the Royal Military College in Sandhurst, providing the very bedrock of future success. At the turn of the twentieth century, it is perhaps rather alarming to note that this prestigious seat of military learning still taught the infantry how to form a square and receive advancing cavalry,[2] as Wellington had done at Waterloo back in 1815. Change, innovation and modernisation soon followed, by necessity, although many of the principle architects of strategy in the First World War, including Douglas Haig, Edmund Allenby, Horace Smith-Dorrien and Henry Rawlinson[3] had long since left the classroom before embarking

1   Lord Kitchener was the Secretary of State for War whose famous 'Your Country Needs You' recruiting posters were distributed across the UK. The authorities were overwhelmed by the numbers responding to the call, and by the end of September 1914, it was estimated that 750,000 had enlisted.
2   Thomas, H, *The Story of Sandhurst* (London: Hutchinson 1961), p. 163
3   Field Marshal [in 1917] Sir Douglas Haig is one of the most controversial figures of the war. Commander-in-Chief of the British army from October 1915, until the end of the conflict, he oversaw the offensives on the Somme (1916) and Passchendaele (1917) before the eventual triumph of 1918. He is viewed by historians mainly either as a callous

upon their army careers in far-flung outposts of empire. From 1914 onwards, they, too, had to change, innovate and modernise their own attitudes towards command, with results which still divide and antagonise opinions in many different spheres.

When war broke out, Sandhurst focused primarily, and understandably, upon the sole business of training cadets for combat. Many officers did not even set foot inside its historic buildings, and instead received their training at the numerous army camps which had been constructed across the country. The 19th Division, for example, was stationed on Salisbury Plain in Wiltshire, but it did not even receive its khaki uniforms until March 1915. Manoeuvres, close-order drills, marching and weapons instruction were all focused upon until the division was inspected by His Majesty the King three months later – usually the pre-cursor to a posting overseas.

On the eve of its deployment to France, the composition of the 19th (Western) Division was as follows:

19th Divisional Headquarters
19th Divisional Artillery HQ; 86, 87, 88 and 89 Brigades, Royal Field Artillery
19th Divisional Royal Engineers HQ; 81, 88 and 94 Field Companies, RE; 19th Divisional Signal Company. C Squadron, Yorkshire Dragoons. 19th Divisional Cyclist Company.

56 Infantry Brigade:
   7/King's Own Royal Lancaster Regiment.
   7/East Lancashire Regiment.
   7/South Lancashire Regiment.
   7/Loyal North Lancashire Regiment.
57 Infantry Brigade:
   10/Royal Warwickshire Regiment.
   8/Gloucestershire Regiment.
   10/Worcestershire Regiment.
   8/North Staffordshire Regiment.
58 Infantry Brigade:
   9/Cheshire Regiment.
   9/Royal Welch Fusiliers.
   9/Welch Regiment.
   6/Wiltshire Regiment.

butcher or a brilliant strategist. Field Marshal [in 1919] Sir Edmund Allenby had mixed successes on the Western Front before gaining plaudits for his capture of Jerusalem in 1917. General Sir Horace Smith-Dorrien was involved with the first twelve months of the war, notably a gallant stand at Le Cateau in August 1914, until relieved of his command by General Sir John French, Haig's predecessor. General [in 1917] Sir Henry Rawlinson commanded the British Fourth Army at the Battle of the Somme in 1916. He has been widely criticised after the first day, and his contribution is featured later in this book.

[NB: The twelve infantry regiments listed above are inscribed on the 19th Division Memorial, opposite La Boisselle Church, depicted in Figure 1.1]

5/South Wales Borderers (Pioneers)
57, 58 and 59 Field Ambulances.
154, 155, 156 and 157 Companies, Army Service Corps.
31 Mobile Veterinary Section.
19th Divisional Supply Column.

In command was Major-General CGM Fasken, who had spent much of his career in India.

The army structure can be broken down as follows, although numbers have been generalised, as the larger figures invariably differed at any given time during the war:

Division: 12,000 – 14,000 soldiers
Brigade: 3,000 – 4,000
Battalion: 800 – 1,000
Company: 160 – 200
Platoon: 40 – 50
Section: 10 – 14

The battalion strength, for example, could be severely depleted during a major offensive, or by the outbreak of an illness. A battalion was commanded by a colonel or lieutenant colonel, with a major as his second-in-command. A captain or lieutenant was usually in charge of a company, with a second lieutenant taking responsibility for a platoon.

Again, in times of battlefield losses, these hierarchies could change, and sometimes a junior subaltern would find himself as the most senior rank left to lead an attack when all of his superiors had been killed or wounded.

As the 19th Division prepared for its mass exodus across the English Channel at the end of July 1915, seasoned veterans of the Western Front were also in the process of a relocation. Soon, they would find themselves in trenches once occupied by the French, and, in places, within yards of the German positions. They were not far from the River Somme; the village which lay opposite was called La Boisselle.

Part I

Preparations

1

La Boisselle: An Obscure Battlefield

In 1914, the village of La Boisselle had no strategic value. It was not the gateway to a major geographical or military prize, nor did it possess any vast mineral stores, such as much needed coal for the transport of troops and ammunition. It was not a major rail centre, or a significant garrison, or even a place which stirred the patriotism of some past glory in battle. It was, very simply, one part of rural Picardy where two armies collided in the autumn of 1914 and remained deadlocked for almost two years.

The surrounding landscape, which was (and still is) mainly agricultural, consists of rolling chalk-land fields, punctuated by small woodlands. The village sits on the old Roman road between the nearby market town of Albert, to the south-west, and smaller Bapaume, to the north-east. The latter location was the scene of a battle during the Franco-Prussian War of 1870–71, after forces from Prussia – allied with other German states – invaded France following some blatant political manoeuvring which made conflict inevitable. Victory was overwhelming for Teutonic strategy and military might, directly leading to the unification of Germany as a powerful and ultimately

Figure 3.1 The villages of Ovillers and La Boisselle today. (Author's collection)

threatening empire in its own right. The consequences of this short but brutal conflict sowed the seeds for future foreign policies from both countries, setting in motion the inexorable slide towards further instability and mistrust.

Older inhabitants of the region harboured long and bitter memories about the outcome, whilst the looming spectre of the colossal struggle which many expected to break out in Europe sooner or later became more ominous with each passing year.

La Boisselle itself sits on a spur of land, and the modern village rises from a shallow dip (which was virtually the position of the British front line on 1 July 1916) up towards Pozières Ridge. (In 1914, this 'dip' was not inhabited by troops, as it was boggy ground and therefore considered an unwise venture to occupy such precarious footings. The closest building was a farm (see Figure 3.3) which was to become a hotly disputed location between 1914 and 1916).

It is interesting to note that at the beginning of the war, the main cluster of houses in the village was centred around the church, on the Contalmaison road, and only a handful of dwellings were situated along the main Albert-Bapaume route. When the village was re-constructed after the war, both thoroughfares were built upon equally.

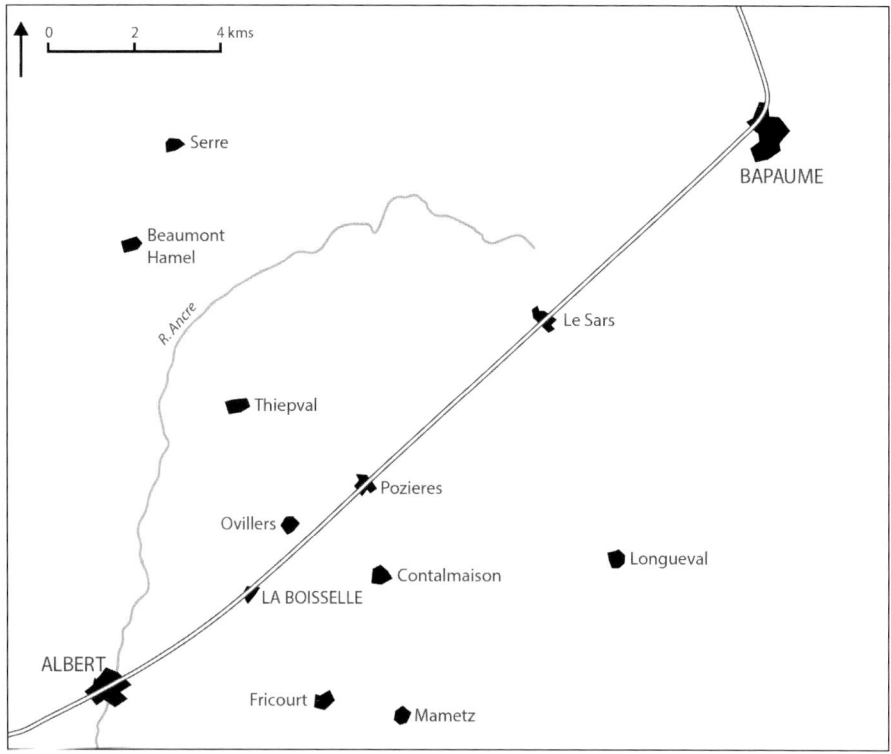

Figure 3.2 A simplified map of La Boisselle and environs. All of the designated place names, apart from Albert and Bapaume, are Picardy locales associated with the 1916 campaign.

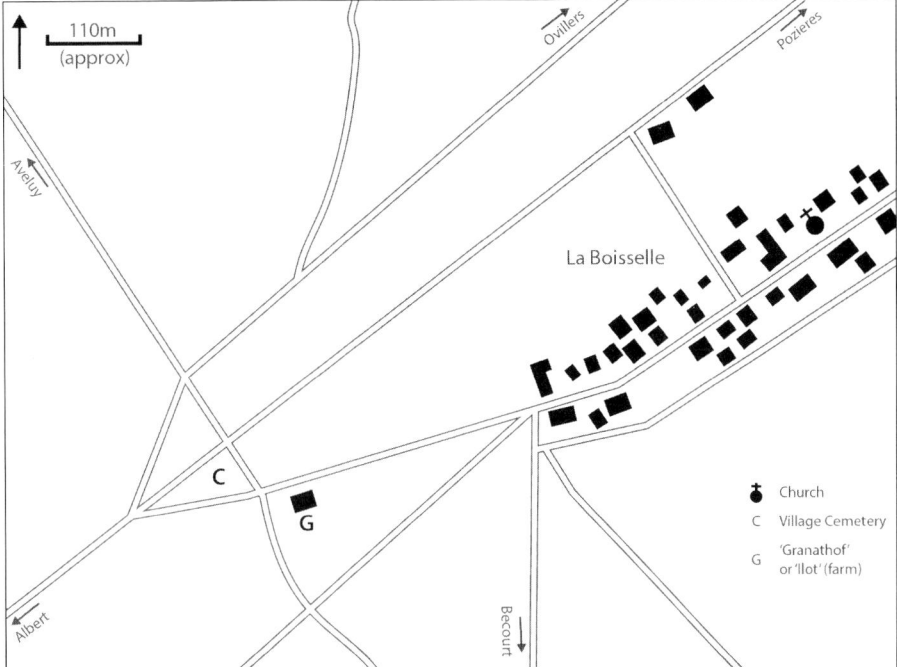

Figure 3.3 La Boisselle and vicinity.

The buildings of neighbouring Ovillers, (technically speaking known as Ovillers-la-boisselle) and La Boisselle itself were completely obliterated by artillery shells in the run-up to the Somme offensive of 1916.

Figure 3.3 shows the *approximate* positions of the houses in La Boisselle from 1914, as well as the roads and paths of the time. The track which runs virtually parallel to the Albert/Pozières road, eventually leading to Ovillers, no longer exists. It is now open farmland, and in 1916 was referred to as 'Mash Valley' by the British. To the south-east of the village, another geological feature which was lower than La Boisselle became known as 'Sausage Valley'. These rather quaint Anglicised nicknames were to become scenes of appalling bloodshed in early July 1916.

When the German invaders took stock of the newly-captured hamlet of La Boisselle in late September 1914, they noted that the majority of the brick-built structures contained strong cellars. To avoid paying window tax, the French had ensured that their barns faced the road, whilst the living accommodation was situated at the rear. The village commanded views over the plateau to the north-west and south-east (including the soon-to-be-christened 'Sausage' and 'Mash' valleys), and in a south-westerly direction rose the road towards the town of Albert, the conglomeration of which was mainly hidden by the brow of a hill.

Figure 3.4 Rue de Bapaume, Albert (1). (Author's collection)

Figure 3.5 Rue de Contalmaison. (Author's collection)

The civilian cemetery was situated where the two roads diverge at the foot of the incline [marked 'C' in Figure 3.3], although its modern equivalent is now to be found a short distance away, on the corner of the northern boundary of the Aveluy road, and the main Albert/Pozières route. Its original counterpart was also the site of much bitter fighting, and the once peaceful burial ground was soon swallowed up by the trenches.

   This brief summary provides the backdrop for future events at La Boisselle, the inhabitants of which – who were driven out of their homes – could never have predicted the devastation which was to follow.

Two pre-war images: Figure 3.4 – 'Rue de Bapaume, Albert'. This Roman road led directly out of the town, through La Boisselle, and on towards Bapaume. Figure 3.5 – The main street of La Boisselle itself. This particular image was sent as a German Feldpostkarte by a soldier of *XIV Reserve Corps* in early February 1916. By this time, the buildings had been destroyed by sixteen months of persistent shelling. The church in the background gives a perspective as to the general location (See Figure 3.3).

2

Early Battles: August 1914 – July 1915

From a British perspective, the early fighting of the Great War is understandably focused around the areas in which the first contingent of the British Expeditionary Force engaged the Germans following the United Kingdom's entry into the conflict on 4 August 1914. Four days earlier, Kaiser Wilhelm's armies had crossed the border into Belgium with their eyes on the greater prize of the French capital, Paris, and thus with neutral territory violated, Britain and her considerable empire was mobilised.

To summarise briefly (and not do justice to the heroics of the French, Belgian and British forces involved), the German army swept westwards into Belgium before turning south during mid-August, and the BEF first encountered the enemy at Mons in Belgium on the 23rd. (It should also be noted that German soldiers crossed the national border between Germany and France along almost its entire length to Switzerland, although the crux of this narrative is centred solely upon events in northern France and Belgium). Numbering approximately 80,000 strong, including cavalry, the British held the left flank at Mons, and contributed to an estimated strength of 700,000 men (the French Fourth, Fifth and Sixth Armies represented the bulk of this total) waiting to repulse the invaders. The German comparison was over 750,000.

Both France and Germany contained numerous conscripts in their ranks, whereas the BEF was an entirely volunteer force, highly trained and extremely professional, with veterans of various colonial conflicts still serving (or recalled from the reserve) to offer a wealth of military acumen. Despite a spirited fight at Mons, the BEF was gradually driven south, and a brave stand at Le Cateau three days later enabled a large proportion of their retreating comrades to gain some breathing space.

From the end of August until the first week of September, the British – commanded by Field Marshal Sir John French – found themselves sandwiched between the French Sixth Army to the west, and the French Fifth Army to the east. After bitter fighting across the River Aisne, the Germans came perilously close to their goal of reaching Paris, but then a determined Allied counter-attack pushed the Kaiser's men back across the River Marne. A swift and decisive German victory on the Western Front had been thwarted, and with the Kaiser also engaging the Russians on the *Eastern*

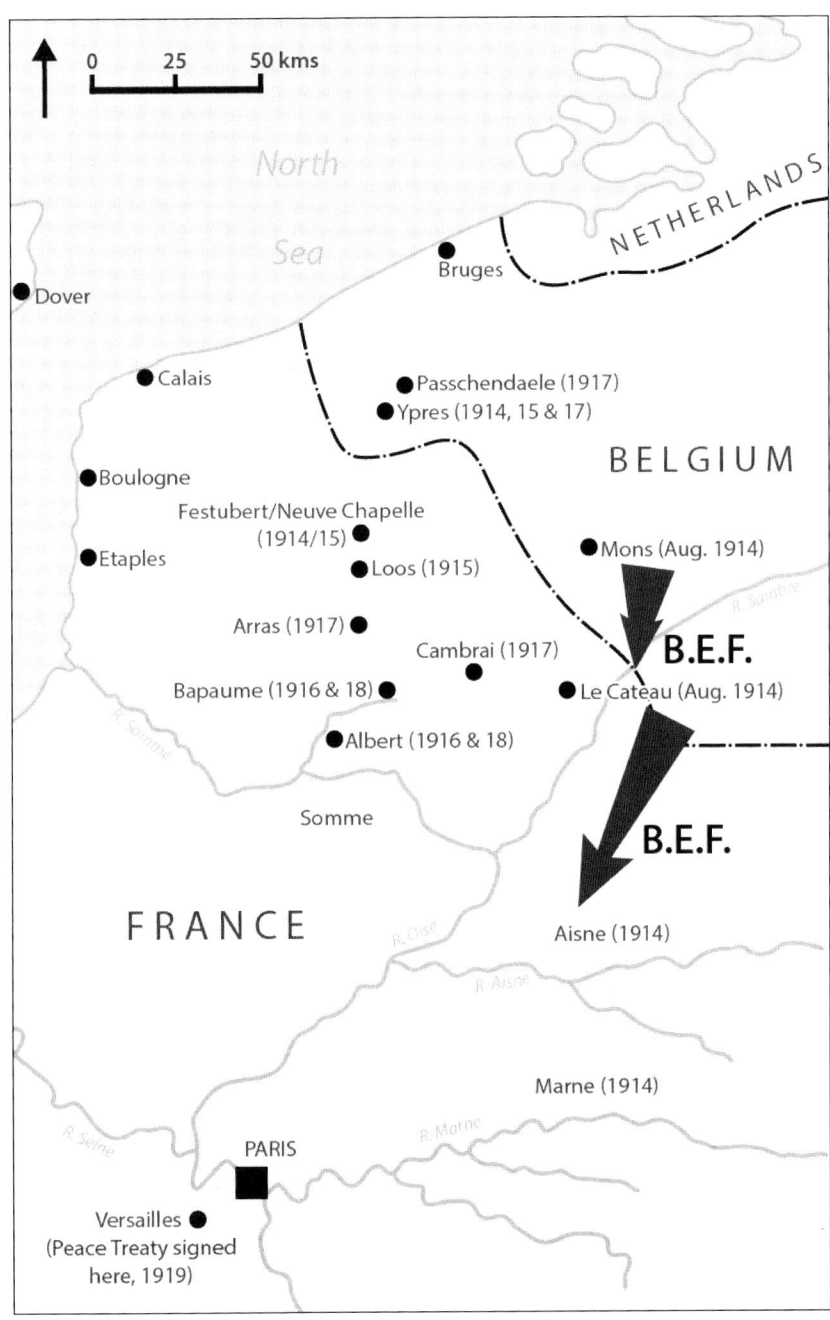

Figure 4.1 The retreat of the BEF in August/September 1914, and the sites of other major battles involving British and empire troops 1914-18

Front, his resources of manpower and equipment were severely stretched. A re-think of strategy was needed, with their thoughts turning to consolidation and defence.

However, we now turn our attentions to the region around Bapaume – away from the so-called 'Miracle of the Marne' – which was held entirely by French troops. German reinforcements were being brought in by train to nearby Cambrai, and on 27 September, Bapaume itself was the scene of heavy fighting, supported by machine-guns and artillery weapons on both sides. French cavalry units were also active, but they could not stem the tide of the German advance, which was continuing along the Roman road towards the village of Flers, led by advanced skirmishing groups. French support troops moved north-eastwards from Albert to meet them, accompanied by aircraft, and sporadic encounters went on into the afternoon. Orders had been received that the leading units of the German *26th Reserve Division* were to reach Ovillers-la-Boisselle by the evening and rest there overnight. It was already dark when Pozières was occupied after a fierce hand-to-hand bayonet duel, and it was then decided to set up camp here until morning.

The following day (28 September 1914) dawned damp and misty. A concerted attempt was made to capture Contalmaison, with the left-wing of the German column using the church steeple as its directional guide. Meanwhile, the remainder moved off towards La Boisselle, crossing flat ground which was strewn with French dead. Heavy resistance was encountered as the German troops reached the top of the incline which then dropped down into the village, and close-quarter combat was again necessary, although this time it was undertaken in broad daylight. The French were determined to hold on to the village, and some of the buildings were set on fire during the mayhem. (It was also during this phase that a terrified goat, with a rooster on its back, began running backwards and forwards between the opposing lines on the main street, unable to escape the noise and confusion. Both unfortunate creatures ended up in German hands where the rooster died, whereupon it was later stuffed and mounted for the barrack room as a reminder to the veterans who fought at La Boisselle).

Despite the French sending fresh soldiers into the fight, the hamlet was eventually cleared by 5 pm, although the isolated farm close to the old civilian cemetery had caused a number of problems to the attacking force, being the only building for several hundred metres which afforded shelter to its defenders.

The hand-painted image [Figure 4.2 – author's collection] is something of an anomaly. It is a German *Feldpostkarte*, sent in April 1916 by a member of 26 Reserve Division, and on the back is written in pencil 'La Boiselle, Granathoft'. The German name for the farm mentioned previously was the *Granathof*, although the presence of non-military graves in the vicinity suggests this was the result of the artist's 'poetic licence', as the civilian cemetery was actually a short distance away, across the lane. The archway in one of the remaining walls is also reminiscent of a church (the religious centre of the village was, in fact, surrounded by other houses further up the road), so this may not be an accurate depiction of the site itself. It is, however, an interesting piece of La Boisselle's war-time history.

Figure 4.2 German watercolour of infamous Granathof. (Author's collection)

The battles on the flanks of La Boisselle, at Ovillers and Fricourt, continued, and the fires lit up the night sky in both directions. These were often caused by French artillery which had retaliated once their infantry had been ejected from each location. The garrison occupying Ovillers had also withdrawn, and the Germans assumed their advance would soon continue. (It is to be remembered that at this early stage of the war, entrenchment and stalemate was not envisaged. La Boisselle was just another village which, it was believed, in several weeks would be many miles behind the German front line). The next step was to encircle Albert, but information had been received that the French were pouring reinforcements into the town to counter such a threat, so it was decided to consolidate the newly taken positions. Rudimentary trenches had already been dug in parts of the line on both sides, affording some manner of respite from the incessant rifle-fire and shelling [Figure 4.3 – author's collection].

The French soldiers holding the *Granathof* were finally driven out on the 30th, and the Germans prepared for orders to move towards Albert at any moment, although to their surprise, they were told to stay put in La Boisselle. Initially, they did not prepare any further trenches, and merely utilised the existing houses and cellars as protection against enemy fire. Overnight, however, the French were industrious with their *own* trench digging, and the occupants of La Boisselle slowly began to realise they might have a longer stay than expected. As the Germans dug down, they soon hit a mixture of rock and hard flint, damaging their tools, and even though their artillery could reach Albert with ease, their French counterparts could be just as ruthless and accurate. Gradually, Ovillers and La Boisselle began to disintegrate under incessant

Figure 4.3 Trench running through La Boisselle. (Author's collection)

Figure 4.4 Early German
trench at La Boisselle.
(Author's collection)

artillery fire, and its defenders (as they had now become) increasingly took cover in the ready-built caverns below ground, as well as beginning to construct their own even more elaborate shelters. [The sketch in Figure 4.4 – author's collection – depicts an early German trench within the ruins of La Boisselle].

With the advent of an operating saw mill in Bapaume, the Germans were able to supply their outlying front-line positions with the much needed resource of wood to shore up the defences, as well as providing heat for cooking fuel as the cold weather set in. The longer nights and foggy mornings provided opportunities to expand, improve and deepen the trenches without the harassment of enemy shells and snipers. Communication lines were constructed to enable troops and supplies to be brought up in the absence of similar threats, and an entire subterranean network was now taking shape. (Another aid to the spotting of intruders in the dark came in the form of a searchlight, which was switched on at random across no man's land, with marksmen ready to fire at any silhouette, before it was extinguished and moved to another location for fear of an artillery bombardment).

In late November, a new and menacing facet of warfare established itself on both sides of the divide. The French pioneers were the first to dig a narrow, shallow trench (known as a 'sap') towards the *Granathof* with the intention of placing explosives underneath it, thus providing the element of shock and surprise to be exploited by a rapid infantry attack immediately afterwards.

Figure 4.5 Another pencil sketch of La Boisselle, dated 15 December 1914.
(Author's collection)

Just two days after the image in Figure 4.5 was drawn, the French launched a major attack between Thiepval and Ovillers, sending five regiments into the fray. The hollow to the north of the Albert/Bapaume Road, facing Ovillers, was heavily waterlogged, and the Germans were well aware of the intentions of the men opposite. Having constructed wire entanglements in front of their own positions, the machine-gun teams easily dealt with the French assault, which included cavalry. One German observer estimated that out of 3,000 who advanced, 2,500 were killed or wounded within the space of twenty minutes.[1] (Their bodies were still on the battlefield the following March, when this soldier's regiment was withdrawn). The carnage was inflicted by two machine guns situated 'on the tip of La Boisselle', close to the old civilian cemetery. (Shortly afterwards, a group of French prisoners of war informed their captors they had given the German regiments holding the village the nick-name 'the devils of La Boisselle').[2]

The French did manage to storm the cemetery on 17 December, albeit after the Germans had found holding the position untenable in the weeks preceding the attack and finally decided to withdraw to the nearby *Granathof.* The cemetery was so close to the French lines, and had been subjected to all manner of grenades and explosives thrown in its direction, that it was causing too many casualties. At noon on Christmas Eve, a hurricane of fire landed on the *Granathof* and its environs, killing or incapacitating almost every German on sentry duty, whereupon a large attacking force seized the position virtually unopposed. Spurred on by their success, the French continued up the main street but were met by withering fire from machine-guns, rifles and a field gun situated within the ruins of the church. The French endeavours were thwarted, and the survivors returned to dig a new trench between the *Granathof* [Figure 4.6 – author's collection] and the cemetery.

Close to midnight, between Christmas Eve and Christmas Day, a retaliatory bombardment rained down upon the new tenants of the *Granathof,* causing more death and misery, and even before the Yuletide was over, plans had been drawn up to re-take the position, but on Boxing Day, assisted by mortars and grenades, the Germans failed to snatch the *Granathof* back. As 1914 ended, the Germans set about turning La Boisselle into a fortress, whilst the French could clearly be heard digging mines towards their trenches. 1915 would see no let-up in the bloodshed.

One major innovation which the Germans began this year was the construction of deep and well-protected dugouts, completely hidden from any enemy observer. These were to prove crucial on 1 July 1916, when the British launched their own major offensive at La Boisselle. In the meantime, the number of sandbags, barbed wire obstacles and other methods of defence were strengthened accordingly. But of initial concern to those in the firing line was the issue of mine shafts. The Germans blew their first

1   Whitehead, Ralph J, *The Other Side Of The Wire: Volume I* (Solihull: Helion & Company, 2010), p. 141.
2   Ibid. p. 149.

Figure 4.6 Trench line
between La Boisselle
and Granathof.
(Author's collection)

Figure 4.7 Believed to be the ruins of La Boisselle, winter 1914/15. (Author's collection)

venture at the beginning of January, intending to dislodge the French from the cellars of the *Granathof*, but their calculations had been inaccurate, and instead destroyed a portion of their *own* trenches. It was believed that crack snipers were using the location to pick off German troops, so it became a matter of urgency to seize the ruined farm as soon as possible.

The Germans had an inferior supply of artillery shells, however, and were often at the mercy of prolonged and damaging bombardments from an enemy whose own stock seemed inexhaustible. In order to prevent the French from further mining ventures, the defenders of La Boisselle tried, unsuccessfully, to negate the *Granathof*. One mine explosion on 11 January apparently set off a French counter-mine, causing a large blast and literally blowing a number of severely wounded French soldiers into no man's land, in front of German lines. A truce was called in order to retrieve the unfortunate men, before the fighting began again.

A week later, yet another German assault finally succeeded in driving the French out of the *Granathof*, whereupon the cellars beneath the building were blown up, destroying in the process a series of tunnels which were pointing towards La Boisselle. A similar operation on 7 February caused further damage, but it did not stop the French activities completely. The occupation of newly formed craters was deemed strategically important, as well as, inevitably, becoming a highly dangerous manoeuvre. Sometimes it was simply a ruse to get the enemy to occupy a recently formed hole in the ground, only for a *second* mine to be detonated once they were in position.

The ruins of La Boisselle were being systematically erased from the ground. One German soldier recalled how the bodies of his dead comrades – which numbered over a thousand – had to be dug up and re-interred at nearby Pozières,[3] as the French shelling was so destructive. By Easter, only a few stones of the church walls remained as a recognisable landmark [Figure 4.8 – believed to be La Boisselle church, early 1915, author's collection] – the rest of the village, including all vegetation, had been damaged or destroyed altogether. The Germans were being bombed or sniped constantly, night and day, yet it did not diminish their resolve.

Their mines now had tunnels of fifty metres long, and seven to eight metres underground, where they were relatively safe from French artillery shells. There were also side corridors, running parallel to the main shaft, which offered a potential escape route should the main chamber collapse, as well as increasing the likelihood of discovering a French counter-mine.

But there was about to be a significant change for those who inhabited this 'hell on earth', as it was described by veterans of the time. At the end of July 1915, a new and uninitiated band of men was about to take over the trenches at La Boisselle, and they wore not the *horizon bleu* uniform of the French, but the khaki favoured by the British.

3   Ibid. p. 214.

Figure 4.8 La Boisselle church early 1915. (Author's collection)

Figure 4.9 A modern, aerial view of the 'Glory Hole', and the south-western fringes of La Boisselle. The craters caused by mining and counter-mining can clearly be seen. The French, succeeded by the British, occupied the trenches to the left, just yards from their German adversaries to the right. (Photo courtesy and copyright of Jeremy Banning <www.jeremybanning.co.uk>)

3

The Role of the British Army Officer and the Journey to the Front

---

It may seem a cliché and a generalisation that those members of the social strata of pre-1914 Britain who received a sound education, usually but not exclusively at a public school, followed by further high learning at any number of national colleges or universities, were more likely to seek an officer's commission at the outbreak of war. It was generally perceived that 'gentlemen' would make ideal moral and confident leaders of men, whilst those further down the class structure *expected* this natural order of things to occur as predicted. The latter group of the working masses invariably left school when they had barely reached their teens, unable to read and write (although this in itself was not seen as a hindrance to their progression in society), and often their sole intention was to provide for their families during harsh economic times.

For those deemed more fortunate, a thorough schooling provided the basis for their eventual career decisions in banking, law, politics or the church, as well as, ironically, in 1914 and beyond, within the British army in its new struggle with Germany. Pupils learned of patriotism and empire, played team sports such as rugby, cricket and rowing (with their associated benefits of physical prowess, competitiveness, and strategy), and were given the option of joining the previously mentioned Officer Training Corps. Although the OTCs can be seen as merely 'schoolboy warriors', its ethos did imbue a military hierarchy, discipline and basic training for a life in uniform. The public and grammar schools system was also geared towards both leadership and loyalty; the latter to one's *House* initially, and to the school as a whole if representing it on the sports field against a fierce rival. (Those who were boarders appeared to possess, in the main, the most enduring attachments to their place of education).

The decision to enlist at all in 1914 contained many contributory factors, including the much heralded love of King and Country, the pursuit of adventure and glory, the belief in a righteous cause, and, maybe most significantly, as a direct response to the actions of their contemporaries; the majority of whom stepped forward within the first months of conflict. The social stigma of *not* becoming an officer may also have played its part, as individuals were sometimes the victim of snobbery and derision if their

Figure 5.1 A pencil sketch of
a British officer at the Front.
(Author's collection)

military rank did not correspond to their apparent class standing. 'Leaders are wanted more than followers, and officers with individuality most of all'.[1]

In several quarters there was a debate as to whether so-called 'educated men' should join the ranks, or become an officer:

> All of the dangers which your correspondents seem to think dog the steps of a man in the ranks are found in the commissioned ranks too. There is advantage to living in the common herd, you can pick your friends more or less, and associate with those whom you find congenial, while higher up you have to be more or less friends with everyone, and the choice of associates is more limited… In my opinion it would have done a lot of fellows holding commissions a world of good if they had first seen service in the ranks.[2]

1   Sibley, WA, *Wycliffe and the War: A School Record* (Gloucester: John Bellows 1923), p. 293.
2   Ibid. p. 296.

A veteran of the trenches would later comment: 'The experiences I have gained have taught me a good deal, and perhaps the thing which stands out especially in my mind is that some of the finest fellows I have ever met are social nobodies, and that under an exterior of common clothes they carry the hearts of perfect gentlemen'.[3]

A number of new recruits featured in this book did, indeed, join the ranks of a particular regiment, only to receive an officer's commission a short while later. This process also enabled an individual to experience the every day drudgery of a private soldier, so he was better equipped to understand the grumblings of an ordinary Tommy who sometimes became disillusioned with all the fetching, carrying and menial labour involved at the lowest level of the army. It also prompted the following remark by an officer who later served in the firing line: 'The worst part [of active service] is the great responsibility for the safety of the lives of one's men, and things I did not mind doing a bit as a Private, I often hesitate about telling my men to do now, because I feel personally responsible for every one of them'.[4]

Another factor to be considered was the limited available places for new officers within any given regiment, despite the rapid growth of the army as a whole. Many expressed a desire to serve with a particular unit, either via their own county or city affiliations, or by attempting to follow in the footsteps of a family member. Sometimes, 'friends in high places' were called upon to exert their influence upon colonels and other notables with strong connections, but the outcome was not always favourable to the impatient young men waiting for their chance to command.

Once accepted to serve under a specific cap badge, however, the fledgling infantry officers were then expected to acquire their own uniforms, along with all of the necessary equipment needed to carry out their duties in any given theatre of war, although it was not always clear exactly which item would become invaluable, whilst another may prove to be an expensive waste of money. New officers were, nonetheless, granted an allowance by the War Office (usually around £50), which for most proved a sufficient amount to cover the majority of eventualities.

For those who received their commissions directly from civilian status, often from school or university, there then followed an awkward transition when, despite being officer class and therefore looked up to by the men under their command, they were often as unaware of military procedures and expectations as the rest of Kitchener's New Armies. Therefore they needed to learn quickly and adapt responsibly.

After the chaotic influx of tens of thousands of volunteers, a gradual structure and organisation was brought into being, with route marches, musketry drills, trench digging and general tactics all put under scrutiny against the backdrop of waiting; waiting for news of a potential posting overseas. Boredom and sometimes frustration accompanied inevitable apprehension and natural fear; although the two negative human traits were clearly not part of an officer's demeanour in front of his men. Finally,

3   Ibid. p. 297.
4   Ibid. p. 299.

the 19th Division received its orders to leave Tidworth, on Salisbury Plain, and as each train pulled out of the station in mid-July 1915, a regimental band played 'Auld Lang Syne'. Recently promoted to lieutenant, 'Jack' Hoyle, of 7/South Lancashire Regiment (56 Brigade), recalled as they reached the port:

> Instead of the cattle barge I had expected, there was a trim cross-channel steamer waiting for us, straining at the leash … All lights in the train were extinguished the moment we left the carriages, and the men were hustled down the gangway and herded down below with furtive speed. In the few lights that were shown the faces of the officers looked pale and grim as they moved about the darkened deck… It was a night of countless stars. As we cleared the harbour we passed a torpedo boat close by, just a black shape with a trail of foam astern, and judging by the shape of the trail she seemed to be twisting like a snake. The officers went below for some food, and groping down the stairs we trod continually on the men, who perched like flies all about and never seemed to resent our tramplings … All the way as we went was the sinister but seemingly lifeless shape of our escort. Eventually we were sailing between long wooden quays while search-lights blinked at us, and the debarcation officer shouted directions through a megaphone.[5]

Moving inland over the next few days, the men were billeted in villages and farm-steads. Lieutenant Hoyle continued:

> Very slowly we are approaching the guns, faintly heard on still nights – but sitting at my window that looks out over these pleasant fields, I find it quite hard to realise that this is part of the country the Germans have invaded; that the noise and destruction are really going on these comparatively few miles across the corn that was just now golden in the late afternoon… It gives quite a theat-rical effect of being behind the scenes.[6]

Clearly a man of intellect, Jack Hoyle commented in the same letter:

> It was a magical night, absolutely still, with a great moon that turned the corn to silver; the trees stood as if tranced, and then eastward among all that silent beauty, one heard the faint dull percussions, "pup-pup", from along that narrow strip of open ground which the armies have tried in vain during all these months to cross, with an arrested world at gaze.[7]

5   Hoyle, JB, *Some Letters From A Subaltern On The Western Front* (Uckfield: The Naval & Military Press Ltd., & London: Imperial War Museum, reprint, 2009), pp. 12–13.
6   Ibid. p. 17.
7   Ibid. p. 19.

Figure 5.2 British troops on the march, c. 1915. (Author's collection)

Even though the lieutenant had yet to witness the horrors of no man's land for himself, he seemed to have a foreboding about its lethal reputation. Witnessing combat aeroplanes and hearing more cannonades, as well as the troop trains which rumbled past taking other men and equipment to the front, Lieutenant Hoyle was left in no doubt as to the imminence of his own arrival in the firing line. In the meantime, he had daily duties such as the censoring of his men's letters home, in case they inadvertently revealed sensitive military locations. 'Some are well written', the officer noted, 'and quite a number are intimations of regret and hope and affection, that, coming from these outwardly rough people, are very moving'.[8]

In early August, exactly a year after war was declared; Lieutenant Hoyle passed by a major headquarters, and was met with the time-honoured request: "Halt! Who goes there?" by an alert Indian sentry. The incident prompted the former to write: "It struck me afterwards that I should never have thought a year ago I should be walking at the dead of night in France, in the uniform of an officer, and challenged by the voice of an unseen Indian, who gave the familiar formula a chanting note as of an old refrain".[9]

Only a day after the writing of the above correspondence, Jack's brother, Lieutenant Geoffrey Hoyle, of the Sherwood Foresters, was killed in action near Ypres on 9 August. It was to be another week before the surviving sibling received the news as he prepared to undertake reconnaissance close to the German lines.

8   Ibid. p. 22.
9   Ibid. p. 33. Indian troops arrived on the Western Front during September 1914, and despite fighting with distinction, they struggled with the climate. Most had been withdrawn to warmer locations by the end of 1915.

The 19th Division eventually reached the ruins of a village near Merville, close to the Belgian border.

> The buildings loomed strangely in the half-light; on the left was a large church, roofless, with a startling display of daylight through its clerestory windows. On the right was a granary or something similar, with what seemed jagged rents in the walls, and the shutters hanging half unhinged... Coming out again, we passed the farmer and his wife, old, silent and grim – sinister figures in the dawn.[10]

Waiting for his own first taste of action, Lieutenant Hoyle finally heard about the fate of his brother. 'I only wish you wouldn't feel anxious for me', he wrote to his grieving mother, 'I have no anxiety about myself'.[11] He was soon in the trenches: 'It seemed a long time before we were installed behind the bank of sandbags that helps to keep England from Germany. As the flares went up you saw the surprised faces of us new-comers in a weird lime-light setting of light and shade, yellow sandbags, and their grotesque shadows'.[12]

By 2 September, Lieutenant Hoyle and his men had experienced their first bout of enemy firepower:

> At times there is absolute peace and quiet in the trenches; there is an occasional surprise bullet, often not even that; you don't notice them after a while. Also at times a lonely shell passes overhead, crackling and tearing its way to some unseen target behind... A search-light began performing later, and then followed our baptism of fire. A German machine gun, either practicing on some target behind or else searching a piece of ground for possible prey, opened fire in our direction. Lying flat we were quite safe because of the breastwork a few yards in front. But bullets often sound nearer than they are, and to our unaccustomed ears it was us they were looking for with peculiar vindictiveness.[13]

It would be some time before the division received further orders for a re-location to the Somme, so we now return to La Boisselle, where fellow British regiments had already been acclimatising to their own new and hostile environment.

10   Ibid. p. 37.
11   Ibid. p. 41.
12   Ibid. p. 43.
13   Ibid. p. 47.

4

British Occupation of the La Boisselle Trenches (Mines and Raids): July 1915 – June 1916

When 7/Black Watch left the town of Merville in northern France in late July 1915 (where, by coincidence, the 19th Division had just arrived), they were sent on their way with a glowing recommendation from Omer Ducates, one of the officials of the town: *Les Scoths [sic] sans de bon soldats, bien disciplines, aimables et convenables sous tous les rapports avec les personnes. Bons souvenir!*[1]

On 31 July, the men took over the front line at La Boisselle previously occupied by the 19th French Regiment. The sector included the Dohollou Trench, so named after a French officer who was mortally wounded whilst working on that dangerous part of the network, and it was noted in the Black Watch's battalion war diary that this particular location was situated just twenty-five yards from the German lines. Within twenty-four hours of their tenancy, trench mortar bombs had been fired, and an enemy mine was blown at 6:35 pm, wounding one soldier. In the early hours of 3 August, two French mines exploded, blocking several German saps (shallow trenches protruding into no man's land).

On 8 August, two enemy mines were detonated around midnight, the second causing major damage to the parapets, as well as demolishing two British dugouts. These 'tit-for-tat' explosions had become a feature of La Boisselle, and would continue right up until the mass infantry attack on 1 July 1916.

Two weeks later, 179 (Tunnelling Company) of the Royal Engineers took over from the French miners, and on the 26th, following the discovery that the Germans were working in a nearby gallery, close to the *Granathof,* a small mine was set off, although it affected the British shaft as well, incapacitating a number of men who were overcome by poisonous gas. Temporary Lieutenant Herbert Humphreys, of 7/ Black Watch, attached 179 Company, RE, received a Military Cross 'for conspicuous gallantry':

---

1   The National Archives (TNA) WO95/2877: 1/7Black Watch War Diary.

Figure 6.1 The ruins of La Boisselle 1915. (Author's collection)

When two men had collapsed at the bottom of a mine shaft, and although a canary lowered in a cage had collapsed within two feet of the surface, Lt. Humphreys, on arrival, at once descended without any safety apparatus and succeeded in rescuing one of the men. A few days later he attempted a similar rescue, but on this occasion he collapsed and had to be removed to hospital.[2]

(Lieutenant Humphreys was actually recommended for the Victoria Cross for his courageous actions, although the highest decoration for valour eluded him. He later received a Distinguished Service Order for counter-mining against German tunnels in another part of the line, and he survived the war, in time becoming an inspector of coal mines in Yorkshire).

On 14 September, following the detonation of another German mine, more deaths occurred as soldiers rushed to rescue their stricken comrades. Second Lieutenant Cecil Calvert, aged 21, never regained consciousness after he succumbed to carbon monoxide poisoning. Just over a week previously, he had extricated two men from another shattered gallery, digging through the debris with his hands so as not to alert the Germans in an adjacent shaft [Figure 6.2]. His name was put forward to receive a DSO, but he died before the recommendation could be sent to the relevant authorities. His commanding officer informed his family: 'I feel sure it will comfort you to know that he died as he had lived, a victim of his high-souled sense of duty'.[3]

2   *London Gazette*, Military Cross citation, 30 March 1916 (Lt H Humphreys).
3   Various authors, *Deeds That Thrilled The Empire* (Uckfield: The Naval & Military Press Ltd, reprint 2002), p. 678.

Figure 6.2 An incident of the underground war at La Boisselle. (Author's collection)

Figure 6.3 An aerial view of La Boisselle. (Author's collection)

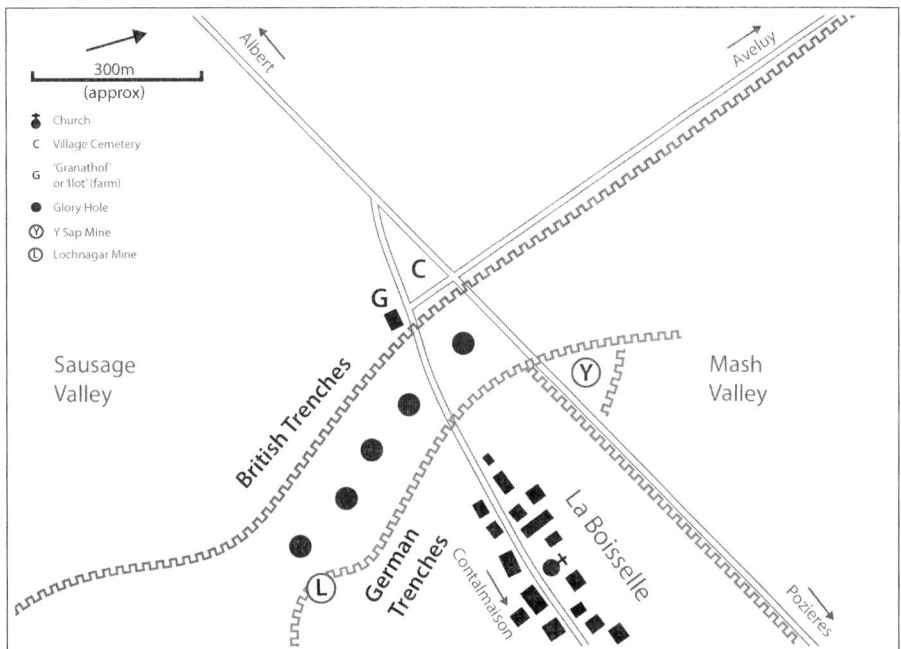

Figure 6.4 KEY: large black dot – Mine craters in No Man's Land. Y: Y Sap. C: Civilian Cemetery. G: Site of Granathof.

The German photograph [Figure 6.3] graphically illustrates the intensity of the fighting at La Boisselle. The mass of white chalk thrown up by the mining and counter-mining from both sides dominates the southern tip of the village, around the *Granathof*, and whilst the road layout is still visible, the trench systems are also prevalent. Y Sap was a trench which protruded into no man's land from the German lines, and is close to the area where so many French infantrymen fell in Mash Valley on 17 December 1914. It is pock-marked with artillery shells, and due to the German front line rising sharply up, and parallel to, the road towards Pozières, it is little wonder the 'apex' of the enemy salient, close to the civilian cemetery, was the scene of almost constant harassment from the French, and then the British, in the trenches opposite.

In November, men of 10/Essex Regiment were holding the line at La Boisselle, and on the 22nd, the battalion war diary stated:

> The enemy exploded a large mine in front of ILOT [the French name for the *Granathof*] forming a crater from the northern point of it for 70' to the south. It killed five bombers in a bombers' dugout… We occupied the near lip of the crater almost immediately, and started making sniper's posts. The force of the explosion filled DOOHOLLOW [sic] for about 50' and completely obliterated the front face of the ILOT. In the daylight it was discovered that the explosion had made

Figure 6.5 One of the most exposed sections of the entire Western Front – trenches at the civilian cemetery in La Boisselle. (Author's collection)

the holding of the crater much easier for us because: 1. The new crater formed a very good cover from view. 2. It gave our snipers a good point of vantage over La Boisselle.[4]

The following day, the same narrative added: 'Our snipers did excellent work during the morning; they spotted four different snipers' posts and accounted for all four men'.[5]

At 11:30 that evening, patrols reported they had heard underground work going on at the northern end of Y Sap, which sounded like timber and iron being driven into the chalk. Meanwhile, a new tunnel had been started by the newly arrived 185 (Tunnelling Company), Royal Engineers, in Lochnagar Street, a front-line trench opposite the German positions to the south-east of La Boisselle. This venture would eventually produce one of the most enduring monuments on the Western Front. Just days before the blowing of the German mine which had caused death and destruction in front of 10/Essex Regiment, British miners had reached the water table – a full thirty-six metres below ground. The complexities and logistics of these shafts, all dug with primitive tools (and sometimes even bayonets to reduce the risk of noise and discovery by rival mining) is quite staggering. The men possessed nerves of steel, not knowing if an enemy explosion would be detonated at any moment, trapping them in

4   TNA WO95/2038: 10/Essex Regt. War Diary.
5   Ibid.

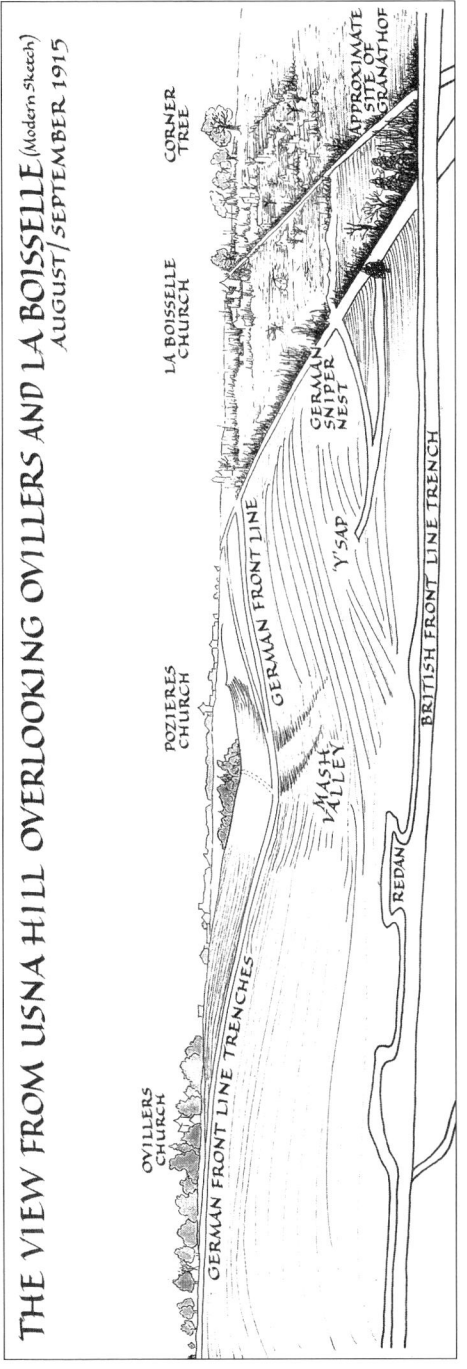

Figure 6.6 Ovillers/La Boisselle sector panorama. (Author's collection)

a collapsed gallery which may then be flooded by poison gas. A number of tunnellers still lie in their ready-made tombs, and any visitor to La Boisselle should pause a while to remember what they went through in such a horrific environment.

By December, the cold, wet and hostile weather was beginning to take its toll. With the trenches full of water (the British, it is to be remembered, occupied the marshy 'hollow' at the foot of La Boisselle), it was sometimes only possible to move around from one location to another above ground, after dark. On the 12th, Second Lieutenant Andrew Knox, of 185 Tunnelling Company RE, was shot in the head by a sniper. His body now lies in nearby Albert. (On 4 February 1916, yet another mine explosion killed two officers – Captain Thomas Richardson, MC, and Second Lieutenant Arthur Latham [see Figure 6.7] – along with eighteen men in the ranks).

Both sides of the wire made regular forays across no man's land in order to gain valuable information as to their foe's intentions, grab a prisoner of war, or simply cause death and injury via a swift sortie accompanied by grenades and the element of surprise. Lieutenant Max Hastings, a former scholar at Wycliffe College in Stonehouse, near Gloucester, recalled:

> The night arrives; nine faces and pairs of hands well blackened, buttons tarnished, identification badges, discs and letters from home left behind, everything that can rattle tied up with string, accompany a roll of tape, a couple of pairs of wire cutters, two Mills bombs per man, nine bludgeons, and, if possible, nine automatics [pistols]. Now there was a professor of languages who went on one of these raids, and he managed to keep silence in seven languages …[6]

A contemporary advertisement of the day, which begins in a quite blunt and overbearing manner, went as follows:

> Little does the 'stay-at-home' realise, as he or she lies comfortably in bed, the hazardous and nerve-breaking work of the man in a trench-raiding expedition. The awful darkness and deathly stillness as he crawls across No Man's Land and the feeling he has become separated from his comrades and lost his way. At times like this the Luminous Compass is a real friend, and has saved the lives of many brave men.[7]

Some individuals, of course, *did* become stranded beyond their own lines, and salvation came in several different ways: 'A week since I was lying out in No Man's Land. A little German dog trotted up and licked my British face. I pulled his German

6   Sibley, WA, *Wycliffe & The War: A School Record* (Gloucester: John Bellows 1923), p. 181.
7   *Cheltenham Chronicle & Gloucestershire Graphic*, 2 June 1917.

tail and stroked his German back. My little friend abolished No Man's Land, and so in time can we'.[8]

> What with inky darkness, pelting rain, knowledge of our isolation, whizzing bullets and bursting bombs, it was very much a question of "What shall we do to be saved?" At this moment there appeared behind us a well-known form, that of our Major. He was quite alone. In his hand was merely a cane, but at the end of the cane was a real man, and something emanated from him which defies definition or analysis. Instantly confidence replaced mis-trust and order supplemented confusion.[9]

A Selection of Officers Who Served at La Boisselle

Figure 6.7 2/Lt A.J. Latham 185 Tunnelling Company, Royal Engineers. Killed by a mine on 4 Feb 1916. (Photograph with thanks to Monmouth School)

Figure 6.8 Captain W.B. Algeo, MC, 1/ Dorset Regt. Took part in a raid on Y Sap in late March 1916 – see following pages. Later killed in action at Thiepval. (Photo with thanks to the Dorset Regt Museum)

8   Sibley, *Wycliffe & The War*, p. 335.
9   Ibid. p. 293.

Figure 6.9 Lt H. Mansell-Pleydell, MC,
1/Dorset Regt. Accompanied Capt Algeo,
MC, in the raid at Y Sap, & died at his side
on 17 May 1916. (Photo with thanks to
Marlborough College)

Figure 6.10 2/Lt N.C. Blakeway, 1/Dorset
Regt. Killed in action during the Y Sap raid
on 27 March 1916 – see below. (Photo with
thanks to Cheltenham College)

Figure 6.11 Captain W.B. Creswick,
attached 179 Company, RE, was killed in
a mine shaft on 10 April 1916. (Photo with
thanks to Giggleswick School)

Figure 6.12 2/Lt P.M. Harte-Maxwell,
attached Royal Irish Rifles, died during
a German trench raid at La Boisselle on
11 April 1916. (Photo with thanks to The
Naval & Military Press Ltd)

In late March 1916, a major raid was undertaken by officers and men of 1/Dorset Regiment, centred upon Y Sap and the trench to its right. Several mines were exploded just after midnight on the 27th, followed by a determined rush from the Dorsets, but the Germans knew of the attack, and had acted accordingly. Y Sap had been deepened, as well as being strewn with barbed wire in the base of the trench, with only a couple of token defenders left to man the position. After a fierce fire-fight emanating from La Boisselle, the British withdrew having failed to secure any prisoners. Second Lieutenant Noel Blakeway [see Figure 6.10] was then reported 'wounded and missing': '[He] was seen lying on the German parapet, and every possible effort was made to remove him, [but] this was found [to be] impossible. Parties were at work assisting to get in the wounded until dawn, a task that was rendered extremely difficult and dangerous by German machine-gun fire'.[10]

Captain William Algeo, MC, [see Figure 6.8] and Lieutenant Henry Mansell-Pleydell [see Figure 6.9], both took part in the operation, and both returned unscathed, only to lose their lives in action during a similar raid at Thiepval several months later. The fate of Second Lieutenant Blakeway, however, is revealed via eye-witness testimonies contained within his service record,[11] and provides an example of how different individuals viewed the same event from a range of perspectives. Lieutenant Goddard recalled: 'Lt. Blakeway was shot. He fell in the barbed wire. A notice-board was put up enquiring from the Germans whether he was still alive or not, and the answer came back he was dead'.

Private Hearn reported: 'The Germans buried him. We asked for his body but they refused to give it up'. Private Moffat claimed: 'The Germans knew it [the raid] was coming off and laid a trap, filling the trench…with barbed wire. Lt. Blakeway was caught in it and could not get out'. Sergeant Webb told the authorities that after the mines had been blown '… we were crawling towards their trenches with Mr. Blakeway leading – by the light of a star shell we saw him wave to us and call on C Company to follow him, then we saw him disappear into the trench and we never saw him again'. Lance Corporal Rawlinson was sure the second lieutenant had been killed instantly by shrapnel – 'I saw his dead body'. Sergeant Webb continued: 'He was a dare-devil, always up to some deal with the enemy, taking their iron plates, etc. On the Kaiser's birthday, the enemy put a paper in front of their trench – Mr. Blakeway went and took it. A fine officer much respected'.

Of the incident with the notice-board, Lance Corporal Morgan believed it intimated that the Germans '… had a trophy in the form of an English officer'. Private Farrell thought it assured them the officer had been buried 'respectably' behind the German lines, whereas Private Duckling was convinced the message read: 'We brought in the vermin and buried him in our dung heap'. Private Channell: 'Lt. Blakeway was a very daring officer. Only the night before he had gone up to the German lines and brought

10   TNA WO95/2392: 1/Dorset Regt. War Diary.
11   TNA WO339/30750: 2/Lt Noel Blakeway service record.

in some trophies. We believe the Germans were on the lookout for him on the next night'.

(With respect to Private Channell's memory of the night attack, it is unlikely the Germans had 'recognised' Second Lieutenant Blakeway as the man who had 'brought in some trophies' during the previous evening. Had they been able to get a close up look at his features, they would surely have shot or captured him there and then). Others were of the opinion that Second Lieutenant Blakeway had gone to the rescue of a wounded lance corporal, and been fatally injured in the process. The officer's body now lies at Martinpuich, near Pozières.

As plans for the summer offensive on the Somme were now well underway, the tunnelling continued at pace. One such shaft was known to be perilously close to a German counter-mine, and Captain Wilfred Creswick [see Figure 6.11], attached to 179 Company, RE, accompanied by a handful of comrades, was caught in the blast when the enemy detonated theirs first. The captain's name is now inscribed on the Thiepval Memorial to the Missing of the Somme.

Knowing a huge build-up of men and artillery was occurring opposite their lines, the Germans launched a series of their own disruptive raids, rushing across no man's land following a fierce bombardment. The 1/Royal Irish Rifles were holding the line on 11 April and telephone communication was cut. Lieutenant Percival Harte-Maxwell [see Figure 6.12], attached from the Connaught Rangers, was killed during this incident, along with a number of other ranks.

Officers and men of the 19th Division were now undergoing rigorous training. Just some of the tasks allotted to them included '… getting out of deep trenches, climbing over walls, bayonet fighting, rapid loading, movement in extended order, organising a company for rapidly placing a captured village or locality in a good state of defence, advancing over open country under shell-fire and distant rifle-fire, during attack and defence the actions of machine guns [are] to be included, intercommunication during battle' and so on.[12]

In May, Lieutenant Jack Hoyle, 7/South Lancashire Regiment, was given a new role in command of a brigade of scouts, so he became somewhat detached from his regular men. He was also sent on various courses, one being '… of general instruction and has no particular reference to Machine Guns, nor am I to deal with those infernal engines'.[13] The officer had also recently been awarded the Military Cross, and he modestly told his family: 'Its chief point for me is the pleasure it brings all of you at home; for myself I can only say that countless others have done so much more, unrewarded'.[14]

12   Wyrall, E, *The Nineteenth Division 1914–1918* (Uckfield: The Naval & Military Press Ltd, reprint 2009), pp. 30-31.

13   Hoyle, JB, *Some Letters From A Subaltern on the Western Front* (Uckfield: The Naval & Military Press Ltd, & London: Imperial War Museum, reprint 2009), p. 214.

14   Ibid. p. 215.

Some units of the division, including the Royal Engineers and the Pioneers (5/ South Wales Borderers) were already assisting the preparations for the forthcoming attack and were in the trenches opposite Ovillers and La Boisselle by the beginning of June. The rest of the infantry was in the region of Amiens, behind the lines to the south-west of Albert.

Meanwhile, two major tunnels were inching their way towards the German front lines, both – as yet – unmolested. One was heading for Y Sap, which had become a thorn in the side for successive British regiments, whilst the other was directed towards a German salient which the enemy called the *Schwaben Höhe*, commanding the higher ground overlooking Sausage Valley on open fields to the south-east of the village. In between both of these shafts was the Glory Hole [Figure 6.13 – looking north-eastwards towards Pozières – author's collection].

The German defenders of La Boisselle had not been idle. They now knew that both Y Sap (known as the *Blinddarm)* and the *Schwaben Höhe* were being targeted by mine tunnels, but they possessed vital telephone communications and listening stations – 'Moritz 28 North' was one of the latter posts located deep underground near the Glory Hole. Crucially, it was intercepting British messages and sending back the information to HQ. The Germans had also rigged up an electricity supply, which lit up their tunnels and enabled them to work longer below ground. Candles, it was soon discovered, devoured much needed oxygen in confined spaces.

With the obliteration of the buildings of La Boisselle more or less accomplished by the efforts of French and British artillery since 1914, their targets had also been making good use of their subterranean world. Whilst the digging of mine shafts inevitably required the need for the disposal of chalk and earth, the deep dug-outs they inhabited – and, indeed, strengthened, deepened and reinforced as time allowed – could be done imperceptibly. The British, of course, knew of the mining activities, and could put certain measures in place to react accordingly, but the shelter provided by the resourcefulness of soldiers waiting for the impending attack had not been factored in to the detailed plans. Though well-entrenched and stoutly defended, the Germans at La Boisselle were considered – as on other parts of the front – to be acutely vulnerable

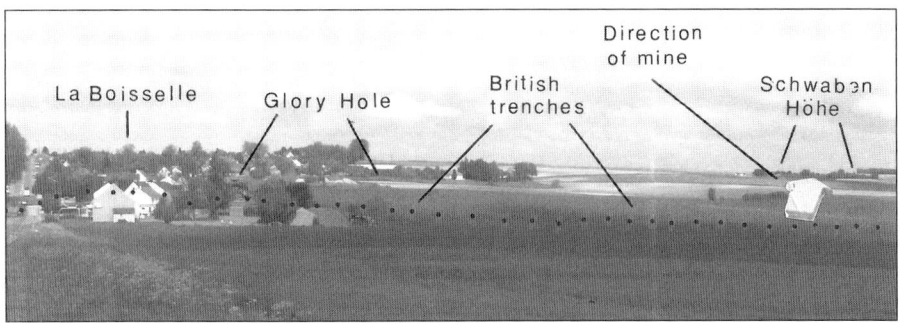

Figure 6.13 The Glory Hole today. (Author's collection)

Figure 6.14 Albert Basilica. (Author's collection)

Figure 6.15 The destructive force of an exploding shell on the Western Front
(Author's collection)

to the forthcoming cannonade which would soon pour down upon them for seven long days.[15] The death and destruction it would render was fearsome and bloody, but it was not to bring about the total annihilation most were predicting.

In June 1916, Lieutenant Jack Hoyle, MC, wrote to his mother:

> Our way led through a town [Albert] that is as remarkable a sight as you could wish to see. The church is gutted, though the tower, chipped in every direction, still sticks up by a miracle; it is topped by a statue, a most lovely and charming piece of work, which still hangs on, but bent right over and pointing down into the street like the tassel of a nightcap...[16]

Two miles away stood the village of La Boisselle, and the officer had just been given the new post of divisional forward observing and liaison officer. He would soon have to cross the murderous Mash Valley.

15   The original plan was for five.
16   Ibid. p. 238.

5

Preparations for the Attack and Events of 1 July 1916

The plan, on paper at least, appeared simple. A massed infantry assault, preceded by a devastating artillery barrage, would secure much, if not all, of the strongly-defended German front-lines, followed methodically by the second and third tier systems, before breaking through to the open ground beyond. A joint Franco-British advance was designed to pit the experienced French soldiers, alongside Kitchener's New Armies, against the tact and awesome depth of the German defences, but the latter had an unsuspecting trick up their sleeve when they launched a major all-out offensive at Verdun (a distance of approximately 137 miles – 220 kilometres – from La Boisselle) in February 1916. The ferocity of the onslaught was matched by the French determination to repel its consequences, and as more and more troops were sent to its aid, it became clear the onus of the forthcoming battle on the River Somme would rest squarely with General Haig's mainly untested divisions.

Some, it was true, possessed recent tales of warfare in Gallipoli, whilst others were regular (ie pre-war units), although many of these regiments had been bolstered by volunteer reinforcements from the early months of the conflict, leaving the vast majority of battalions (such as those in the 19th Division) as having a year of acclimatising in the trenches further north without the experience of participating in such a colossal and exposed movement of soldiers towards the enemy positions.

With Verdun close to buckling under the almost incessant pressure of the titanic German assault, the French call for a British counter-strike to divert attention away from this cauldron became ever more urgent. General Haig had approved of the pre-Verdun scenario, as it allowed his own troops more time to prepare, but this new proposition of entrusting his men to a much greater burden of the attack, and sooner, vexed him greatly. However, he knew he had to comply, and placed General Rawlinson in charge of the Fourth Army, ready to deliver the objective of capturing Bapaume. With the cavalry in reserve, waiting to sweep through any gaps which appeared, the role of the infantry was not to be one of swift movement, but of slow consolidation, moving forward in stages to secure the various lines of German trenches once they had been obliterated by the artillery bombardment.

The date of the assault was fixed for 29 June, and even the time had been specified – 7:30 am. At this time of year, dawn is a full three hours earlier, and the advantages of clear observation to the waiting Germans was obvious. Thus it was paramount that there were *no* waiting Germans left alive at this hour of the morning. Haig requested Rawlinson reduced the length of the barrage to keep the Germans guessing as to the eventual launch of the advance, and he also suggested the enemy trenches were stormed as soon as the shelling ceased. A third compromise was the taking of *two* German lines on the opening day, and not just the cautious one. The latter point was conceded by Rawlinson, and Pozières – sat astride the ridge beyond La Boisselle – was the newly set target by nightfall. Yet the other two areas of discussion were not sanctioned by Rawlinson; nor were they pressed by Haig. It has been a contentious military issue ever since.

So the build-up of men, armaments and equipment on the Somme began in earnest, and the microcosm of events at La Boisselle was repeated up and down the line. Artillery pieces were laboriously dragged into position, training their sights on the trenches opposite (for every seventeen yards, there was one piece of weaponry capable of projecting shells across no man's land),[1] but there was to be a huge psychological blow to hit the preparations, when Lord Kitchener – the architect of the New Armies waiting for their first real taste of action – was drowned on 6 June when the Russia-bound HMS *Hampshire* struck a mine and sank near Scapa Flow. It was a harsh blow for the volunteers, many of whom had joined battalions with a heavy regional bias in the United Kingdom, inspired by Kitchener's recruitment posters and general persona.

The inferno began on 24 June, ready for the infantry to go over as planned on the 29th. Intense shelling of certain areas was interspersed with the harassment of positions further back, assisted by concentrated machine-gun fire, all designed to maximise the chaos and devastation in the German trenches.

> I watched a heavy artillery bombardment directed upon Mametz Wood and Contalmaison [to the south-east and east of La Boisselle]. The mottled sky was flecked with shrapnel puffs and fat black fountains of smoke incessantly spurted from the earth, heralded by preliminary winks of flame. I could distinguish, by my knowledge of where our positions ran, which were our shells, and which were those of the enemy, and it gladdened me to see which preponderance the former were.[2]

As the noise and destruction intensified, witnesses observed: 'The bombardment from both sides then became violent. Some of the Huns took to their heels, and shouted "*Kamerade! Kamerade!*" One of them whined like a dog. We then dug

1   Middlebrook, M, *The First Day On The Somme – 1 July 1916* (London: Penguin Books 1984), p. 87.
2   *Gloucester Citizen* newspaper, 12 July 1916.

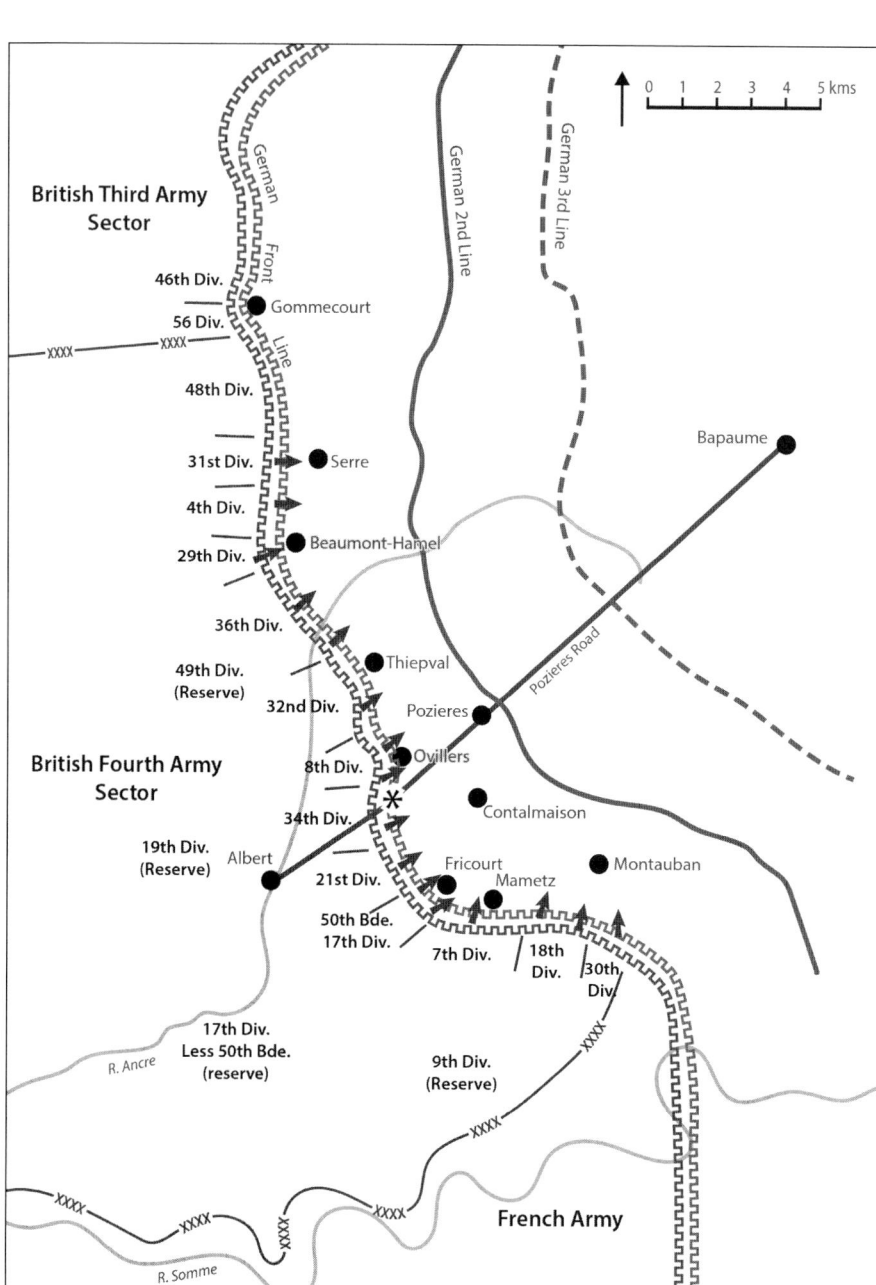

Figure 7.1 The proposed British advance on the Somme. Note the 19th Division was in reserve at Albert on 1 July 1916. La Boisselle (marked thus * on the map) was squarely in the path of the advancing 34th Division.

ourselves in, shells screaming overhead [all] the while…. Some of the Bosches came in and gave themselves up'.[3]

The following report also appeared in one of the newspapers, under the head-line 'Diabolical Treatment of Wounded Officer'. During the last week of June, the captured individual concerned was apparently hauled onto the parapet of an enemy trench after being told: '"You will now see what your cursed bombardment is like". The gallant Huns then descended into their deep dugouts, where I trust and believe they were bombed to extinction by our infantry, who stormed the place soon after-wards, and carried back the wounded officer'.[4]

Other events, which possessed obvious propagandist qualities, included: 'Just before the offensive four dogs came out of the German lines and crossed over to [ours]. The Germans whistled and shouted but the deserters held steadily on… Our men, of course, hailed it as an omen'.[5]

On 28 June, Lieutenant Jack Hoyle, MC, stood on a 'commanding hill to watch the proceedings', probably just outside Albert:

> I was glad to find that from my study of the photographs I picked up the villages, etc., without difficulty. There, right away before us was the War, like a print of some battle of Wellington's [of Waterloo fame]. We saw the shells flash and the columns of smoke rising. Villages that were pounded a little further, and others, where the trees were still green, were getting a foretaste. Uphill and down dale the winding lanes of chalk marked the trenches.[6]

Not all was going to plan, however. The weather had deteriorated, and the decision was made to postpone the assault until 1 July. This, in itself, brought about all manner of logistical problems, including the re-scheduling of the artillery time-table, which now had a further forty-eight hours to cope with, as well as the deployment of the infantry battalions which were destined for the front-line and now had to be tempo-rarily withheld. Raiding parties were sent out to establish the state of the enemy's protective barbed wire and the trenches it was guarding. One such sortie resulted in the death of Captain Harold Price, of the Tyneside Irish, who had successfully bombed a series of German dugouts at La Boisselle, only to find one of his men was missing after the rest had returned to their own lines. The officer went back and was never seen alive again.

Critically, as La Boisselle itself shuddered under the barrage, the telephone wires remained in operation, and in some parts of the German defences, the bombardment

---

3   *Dean Forest Mercury* newspaper, 22 September 1916.
4   *Gloucester Citizen* newspaper, 13 July 1916.
5   Ibid.
6   Hoyle, JB, *Some Letters From A Subaltern On The Western Front* (Uckfield: The Naval & Military Press Ltd, & London: Imperial War Museum reprint, 2009), p. 237.

Figure 7.2 British artillery bombarding the German trenches at La Boisselle prior to the attack on 1 July 1916. (Copyright: Imperial War Museum – Q20)

had failed to obliterate either the razor-sharp web of entanglements, or the men sheltering behind. Some of the British shells were not of sufficient calibre to destroy the underground bunkers in which the Germans took cover, whilst others were incapable of tearing holes in the barbed wire. A significant proportion simply failed to detonate at all. One officer in particular, Lieutenant Colonel ETF Sandys, in command of 2/ Middlesex, tasked with crossing Mash Valley, to the north-west of La Boisselle, was convinced the obstructions in front of Ovillers had barely been touched, and clandestine raiders had not only confirmed this fact, they also heard Germans alive and well close by. Sandys' verbal fears were addressed to his superior, who did not take heed.

There is no doubt the Germans suffered terribly during the week-long barrage, but those who survived – shell-shocked and enraged at the loss of long-standing comardes – must have harboured a deep-rooted and burning desire for retribution when their moment came. Lieutenant Stanley Webber, 1/South Staffordshire Regiment, wrote on the eve of battle:

> Whilst out at the front I have been upheld, strengthened, and made happy by the love of all at home. This has sustained me all through the trials and dangers of warfare, and I only wish I could repay you for your devotion. If it should be my fate to go under, do not grieve for me, for love stretches over death and makes

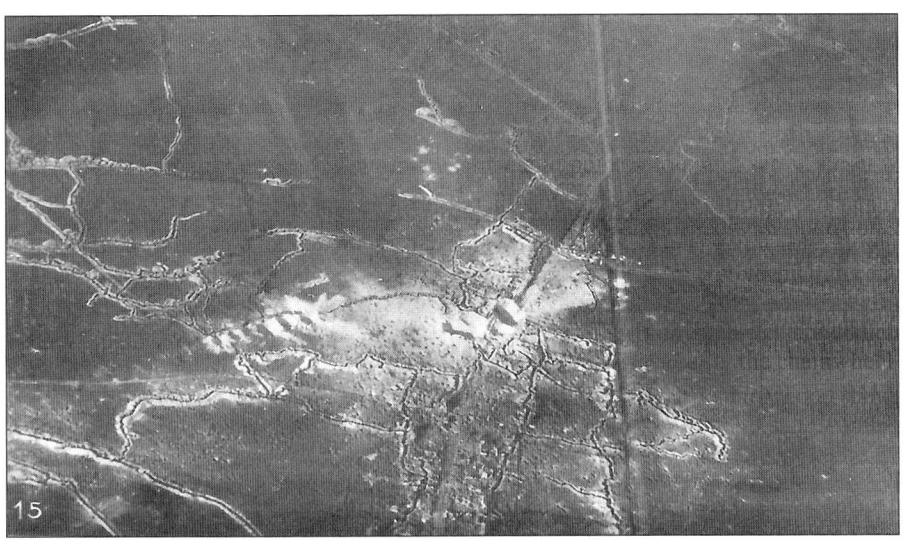

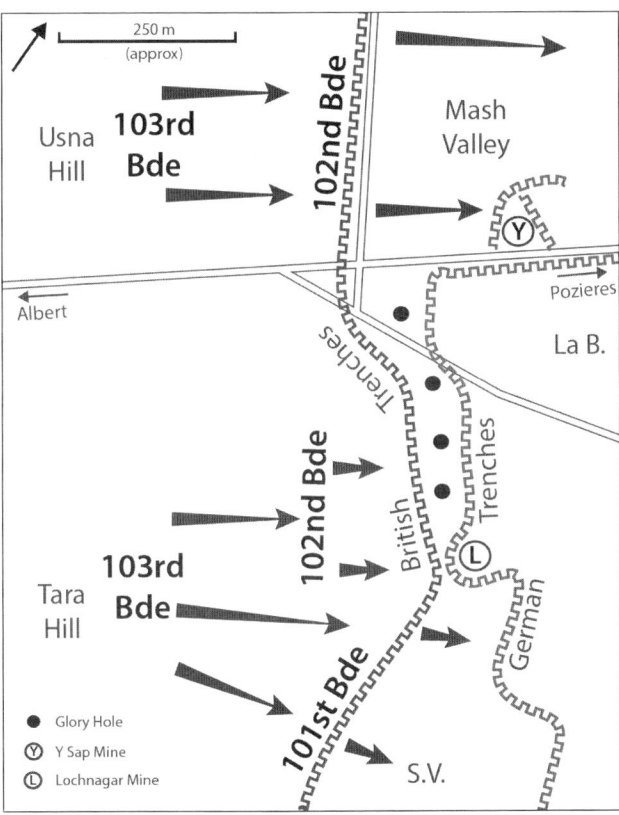

Figures 7.3 and 7.4 The aerial photograph (Figure 7.3: above) was taken in October 1915. For purposes of orientation, the Albert/Pozières road runs north/south to the right of the image. Note the mine craters of the Glory Hole [marked large black dot on Figure 7.4: left] and the intricate German trenches in La Boisselle. On 1 July 1916, as the Tyneside Brigades of the 34th Division prepared to advance, mines at Y Sap [marked Y] and Lochnagar – 'Schwaben Höhe' – [marked L] were blown at 7:28 am. [SV = Sausage Valley]. (Author's collection)

it only a temporary separation. I have no fear of death… [If I fall] I shall leave this world without regret, and glad to have died doing my duty to you all and to my country.[7]

By dusk on 1 July 1916, Lieutenant Webber was dead.

At 6:21 am on the opening day of July, the war diary of 7/South Lancashire Regiment, 56 Brigade 19th Division, noted in somewhat cryptic terms for a normally stark narrative:

> The first shell from a British field gun streaked across the German lines. It was a single prelude note of the immediate opening chorus of the massed guns which lay concealed on every side. The theme swelled from crescendo to crescendo… The day threw into vivid relief the antagonistic contrast between man and nature. Due west, the valley of the Ancre lay hot and perfect in the sun, its eastern slopes stained scarlet with massed poppies swaying in the breeze. Northwards could be seen the trees of Authuille Wood and unblemished to the distant view. South-west appeared the roofs of Albert, and above them the gleaming figure of the Virgin Mother, brooding over the torn and twisted life below. Overhead, the lark ascended to the sky with its morning song. But through the quietness of the day came the constant reiterating rush of shells, and an army hidden in the trenches. [Across] hillside and valley lay men waiting to kill and be killed.[8]

As darkness had fallen the previous night, General Rawlinson had issued a call to arms to his troops, assuring them that the accurate and sustained fire of the artillery during the recent bombardment would greatly assist them in the difficult task which lay ahead. Not wishing for the message to be missed by the men in the forward trenches opposite La Boisselle, a 34th Division staff officer relayed it via field telephone, despite this practice being forbidden due to the close proximity of a German listening post.

At 7:28 am on 1 July, the mines under Y Sap and the *Schwaben Höhe* – either side of the Glory Hole at La Boisselle – were detonated, and the shock waves from both explosions literally knocked men off their feet on the opposite side of no man's land. Hundreds of Germans died at both locations, and as the debris settled, the Battle of the Somme began. (In the Official History of 18/Northumberland Fusiliers, it is noted that even though the mine shafts were fifty feet below each position, the tunnellers quietly digging the last section of the *Schwaben Höhe* chamber could hear the enemy in their nearby dugouts even *further* underground, such was the subterranean shelter created by their foe).

---

7   *The Illustrated Western Weekly News* newspaper, 22 July 1916.
8   The National Archives WO95/2080: 7/South Lancashire Regt. War Diary.

The 34th Division committed all of its brigades – the Tyneside Scottish and Tyneside Irish – to capturing La Boisselle, advancing either side of the Albert/Bapaume Road, leaving the 8th Division to undertake a frontal assault on neighbouring Ovillers. The Germans had positioned their machine-gun nests with a *diagonal* range of fire across the open territory, thus maximising the death zone as the British advanced. Rushing up from their deep dugouts, the defenders of La Boisselle were in position to virtually annihilate the leading waves, even those which had crawled out beyond their own trenches to gain a territorial advantage once the barrage had lifted. Initially advancing in good order, many weighed down with packs and equipment required for the consolidation of newly-captured positions, the British soldiers were systematically mown down as they neared the German lines, easy targets as they bunched together to find gaps in the tangles of barbed wire. Both valleys of Mash and Sausage became hideous killing grounds, strewn with dead and wounded.

Lieutenant JC Reed, Royal Engineers, from Plymouth in Devon, began his advance towards La Boisselle at 7:20 am, from behind the British forward line, and as soon as he cleared the parapet, he was subjected to shrapnel shells and bullets. 'A man behind me sank down with a curious noise, but it did not dawn on me that he was dead as I was too busy thinking about other things'.[9] Somehow, the survivors reached close to the German trenches, and the officer in front of Lieutenant Reed was shot just as he gave the order to lie down. The servant of the former went to bandage him up and was also killed. A party of the enemy then moved closer, but before Lieutenant Reed could close in on them, he was shot and wounded. Two men either side of him fell dead, and the lieutenant took cover behind one of them. He stayed there until 10 pm, whereupon it took him four hours to crawl back to his own lines.

Meanwhile, as the Tyneside Scottish were held up and thrown back at La Boisselle, the Tyneside Irish (all four battalions) had risen up as one and set off from the slopes of Tara and Usna Hills, opposite the village and Ovillers. Marching down the incline [see Figures 7.4 and 8.1] in the wake of their stricken comrades, most did not even reach the original British front line before they had been massacred. Small groups of immensely courageous men pressed onwards, deep into enemy territory, mixtures of Tyneside Scots, Irish, and other remnants fighting forward through unimaginable carnage, until they, too, were captured or killed. One isolated band of men was last seen heading towards Contalmaison, hopelessly outnumbered and facing almost certain death – a quite staggering act of doomed bravery on a day of quite staggering bloodshed. With no reserves to deploy, the 34th Division was a spent force by the afternoon, suffering 6,380 casualties in a single day. (This figure represented over 10% of the entire losses on 1 July 1916 – 57,470 soldiers, of which 19,240 were dead). Officer casualty rates were extremely high along the entire Somme front – three out of four who had gone into action were either killed, wounded, posted as 'missing', or taken

9   *Western Daily Mercury* newspaper, 22 July 1916.

Figure 7.5 German machine-gun teams were highly trained and ruthlessly efficient.
(Author's collection)

prisoner – a final total of 2,438.[10] Of the eight Tyneside Scottish and Irish battalions which attacked La Boisselle, five Commanding Officers lost their lives – Lieutenant Colonel Lyle, 4/Tyneside Scottish, for example, led his men into action carrying only a stick. (Lieutenant Colonel Sandys, who had voiced his concerns about the state of the German wire at the end of June, was wounded in Mash Valley. Traumatised by the loss of so many of his comrades – 540 of his battalion had become casualties on 1 July – he later committed suicide in a London hotel).

Remaining in Mash Valley, the 19th Division was to suffer its first officer fatality in the region of La Boisselle on this most historic and infamous of days. Lieutenant Jack Hoyle, MC, whose journey we have followed from Salisbury Plain to the battlefields of the Somme, had been selected as a forward observing officer, and was attached to the 8th Division:

> As our troops rushed the German trenches opposite Ovillers, your son followed on with an orderly. Half-way across No Man's Land he sent the orderly back with a message, and went on alone. Meanwhile, our troops in that quarter had received very heavy punishment from machine guns, and finally were forced

10   Middlebrook, M, *The First Day On The Somme*, p. 263.

Figure 7.6 Mash Valley and the attack on 1 July 1916 (modern photograph). The British advanced across 700 metres of no man's land, receiving enemy fire from La Boisselle and Ovillers. (Author's collection)

back. Your son, who was seen to enter the German trench, did not return with the survivors of the attack, and that is all we know.[11]

A general staff officer elaborated that telephone communications were attempting to be established in the forward positions, but due to the heavy fire they were experiencing it was not possible to progress very far. Lieutenant Hoyle was seen to press on ahead, towards the German trenches, when his comrades lost sight of him. It is not known which portion of the enemy line he reached, or indeed the time of his death, but a thorough search after dark could find no trace of him. 'In the short time he was with me your son showed himself to be a very good officer, and he certainly acted as a most gallant gentleman in going forward alone into a place where he thought he ought not to take others and risk their lives, yet himself went on according to his orders'.[12]

Born at Knutsford, Cheshire, on 16 September 1892, he was the son of Edward and Margaret, who later lived at Holme Hall in Bakewell, Derbyshire. Educated at a boarding school in Rugby, Warwickshire, he then became a scholar at Pembroke College, Cambridge, in 1911. In September 1914, he was a 'university graduate' when he enlisted in the Royal Fusiliers, spending just seventeen days in the ranks before receiving an officer's commission. After his training, he accompanied the 19th Division to northern France, and was awarded the Military Cross for the following:

On the night of 27/28th February 1916, he and Lance-Corporal Hill made a thorough examination of the enemy wire opposite Neuve Chapelle, crawling about for three hours. He accurately noticed the position and number of enemy sentries, and selected a suitable spot for making a gap in the enemy wire. After returning to our lines and making his report he guided the party to the selected spot and covered them whilst the arrangements were being made. On several occasions Lieut. Hoyle has carried out daring reconnaissances.[13]

Lieutenant Hoyle [Figure 7.7 – The Naval & Military Press Ltd/Imperial War Museum] added modestly in a letter to his mother: 'I still maintain that I had the cushy part of the show, as it was my job to retire discreetly before the scrapping …'.[14] He was presented with his gallantry medal at a parade in late June, just before the artillery bombardment on the Somme began. 'Each recipient advanced, halted a few paces off, saluted, took a step nearer, had the thing pinned on, shook hands, saluted, about turned and rejoined the ranks'.[15]

11   Hoyle, JB, *Some Letters From A Subaltern* … pp. 243–4.
12   Ibid. p. 246.
13   Ibid. p. 160.
14   Ibid. p. 172.
15   Ibid. p. 233.

Figure 7.7 Lieutenant John
(Jack) Baldwin Hoyle, MC 7th
Battalion, South Lancashire
Regiment. Killed in action,
1 July 1916.

Lieutenant Hoyle, MC, was officially declared to be 'missing' by 4 July.
Private Bryant told an enquiry: 'He
was my Platoon Officer for a time and
then became Brigade Scout. He did not
go over with us [7/South Lancashire
Regiment] but I think with the Royal
Fusiliers [he was mistaken, as no RF
battalion was attached to the 8th
Division]. It is reported that his body
was seen in the German lines'.[16]

Other comrades of 7/South
Lancashire Regiment had heard the
same story, including Captain Roland
Garvin (who was killed in action shortly
afterwards) and Private Macafferty.
Corporal Cheetham recalled:

> Lt. Hoyle was attached to the 8th Division as Chief Scout and I understand he
> had been made Captain though I never saw him wearing three stars [there is no
> indication in the records that he had been promoted]. We were at La Boisselle
> on the 2nd July and the 8th Division led the attack [on Ovillers on 1 July]. Lt.
> Hoyle was killed and 2/Lt. Vyner [Rollo Lee Viner] who was killed the next day
> [it was actually on 4 July – see pages 154-155], told me he had seen this happen,
> but he did not give any details. Lt. Vyner [sic] also told me that Lt. Hoyle's body
> had been found but I do not know if it was brought into our lines or not.[17]

(Second Lieutenant Viner's account may not be entirely reliable, as he and Lieutenant
Hoyle were with different divisions on the day, and by the time 56 Brigade, of the
19th Division, was ordered forward towards the British front line near Ovillers on
the afternoon of 1 July, the last known sighting of Lieutenant Hoyle entering the
German trenches had already been reported by the men who had accompanied him
into action).

16   TNA WO339/18099: Lt JB Hoyle, service record.
17   Ibid.

Figure 7.8 Original Great War graves near La Boisselle. (Author's collection)

Ovillers was not captured until mid-July, and Lieutenant Hoyle's body was eventually recovered by burial parties of the Corps Cavalry, which identified him by a leather pocket writing case. The officer, who was aged twenty-three, now lies buried at Ovillers Military Cemetery. Due to Lieutenant Hoyle being attached to another division entirely at the time of his death, his anxious parents could not glean much information from his own regiment, 7/South Lancashires, about the circumstances of his demise. (The body of a Private 'JB Hoyall' was later reported to have been buried at a spot to the west of Ovillers, but as no such individual in the ranks belonged to the battalion, it was assumed he had been mistaken for Lieutenant JB Hoyle. The official confirmation of the lieutenant's death came from the general officer commanding the 32nd Division, which attacked Ovillers from the south-west on 15 July, shortly before it fell to the British).

By the end of the day on 1 July 1916, some gains had been made in the south of the line, but where there were opportunities to press onwards and take further German positions, General Rawlinson held his men back. At La Boisselle, and further north, gallant British attacks had been thwarted by a formidable German defence, and it should be noted that the latter was outnumbered by a considerable margin, so to resist an assaulting force of 120,000 men (along the entire battle-front), inflicting such crushing casualties in the process, was a supreme military achievement. The breakthrough had not occurred, and the first day target of Pozières was still two miles in the distance. The *Ligne de Front 1st Juillet 1916* [Figure 7.9, looking towards Pozières – author's collection] at La Boisselle had barely moved an inch, and 19th Division now faced a most daunting task.

Figure 7.9 Site of front line on 1 July 1916. (Author's collection)

Figure 7.10 The ruins of La Boisselle in 1920. (Gloucestershire Archives D3549/33/2/5)

Part II

The 19th Division Attacks La Boisselle

6

58 Brigade

On 30 June, Major General Bridges, commanding 19th Division, issued the following special order of the day:

> On the eve of a great battle with a treacherous and detestable enemy whose greed of power brought about this bitter war, I wish to remind all ranks of the great things expected of them in the strenuous days before us. Never before has the military situation been so favourable … [Our foe] is now nearing the end of his resources: his material and manhood are alike on the high road to exhaustion. But victory will never be ours until a decisive and overwhelming blow has been dealt to his military forces… I rely with confidence on your courage and grit to uphold the glorious traditions of the British army and of the fine regiments to which you belong, and to make the name of the 19th Division famous in history. Remember we are fighting for the ideal of freedom and the honour of England.[1]

The 19th Division's post-war history observed:

> La Boisselle was a hamlet of some thirty-five houses, lying just south of the main Albert-Bapaume Road … The region had been the scene of much mining activity, and No Man's Land was a confused and tumbled mass of white chalk craters, debris and wire entanglements – a death trap to troops attempting to cross the dread space between the opposing lines… To the naked eye, La Boisselle appeared but a mass of brick and mortar, strewn here and there with the beams and rafters of tumbled roofs. Yet below ground all was different, for beneath the troubled surface, and deep in the bowels of the earth, the enemy had made himself secure. Like the mole he lived underground; he had constructed…vast dug-outs and shelters, often as much as thirty feet down. These were connected,

1   The National Archives (TNA) WO95/2087: 58 Brigade HQ War Diary.

Figure 8.1 The landscape to the south of La Boisselle. On the right are the modern houses at the western tip of the village. In the foreground was the German front line on 1 July 1916, known to them as the 'Schwaben Höhe'. The British advanced across this open terrain and suffered heavy casualties. (Author's collection)

one with the other, by passages, proof against the heaviest shells we could hurl at them.[2]

With the failure of both the 34th and 8th Divisions to jointly capture La Boisselle and Ovillers on 1 July, the 19th Division received orders to move up to the forward positions in anticipation of an attack scheduled to take place at 10:30 pm that same evening, but due to the trenches being heavily congested (and in many cases completely blocked) with a combination of stretcher-bearers, wounded men, assault troops who had expected to be in Pozières by that time, and all of the associated arms and equipment which had to be stored somewhere, the operation was never going to succeed in time.

During the early hours of 2 July, only a portion of 9/Cheshires had reached the old British front line, close to the newly formed crater ('Lochnagar'), and it endeavoured to secure an adjacent German line as well. Later joined by the rest of the brigade, by 4 pm 58 Brigade had deployed, from left to right facing the enemy, 9/Royal Welch Fusiliers, 6/Wiltshires and 9/Cheshires, with 9/Welsh detailed as carrying parties. With a diversionary bombardment taking place on Ovillers, the infantry at La Boisselle – having been told the village must be taken at all costs to enable flanking

2   Wyrall, E, *The Nineteenth Division 1914–1918* (Uckfield: The Naval & Military Press Ltd, reprint 2009), p. 34.

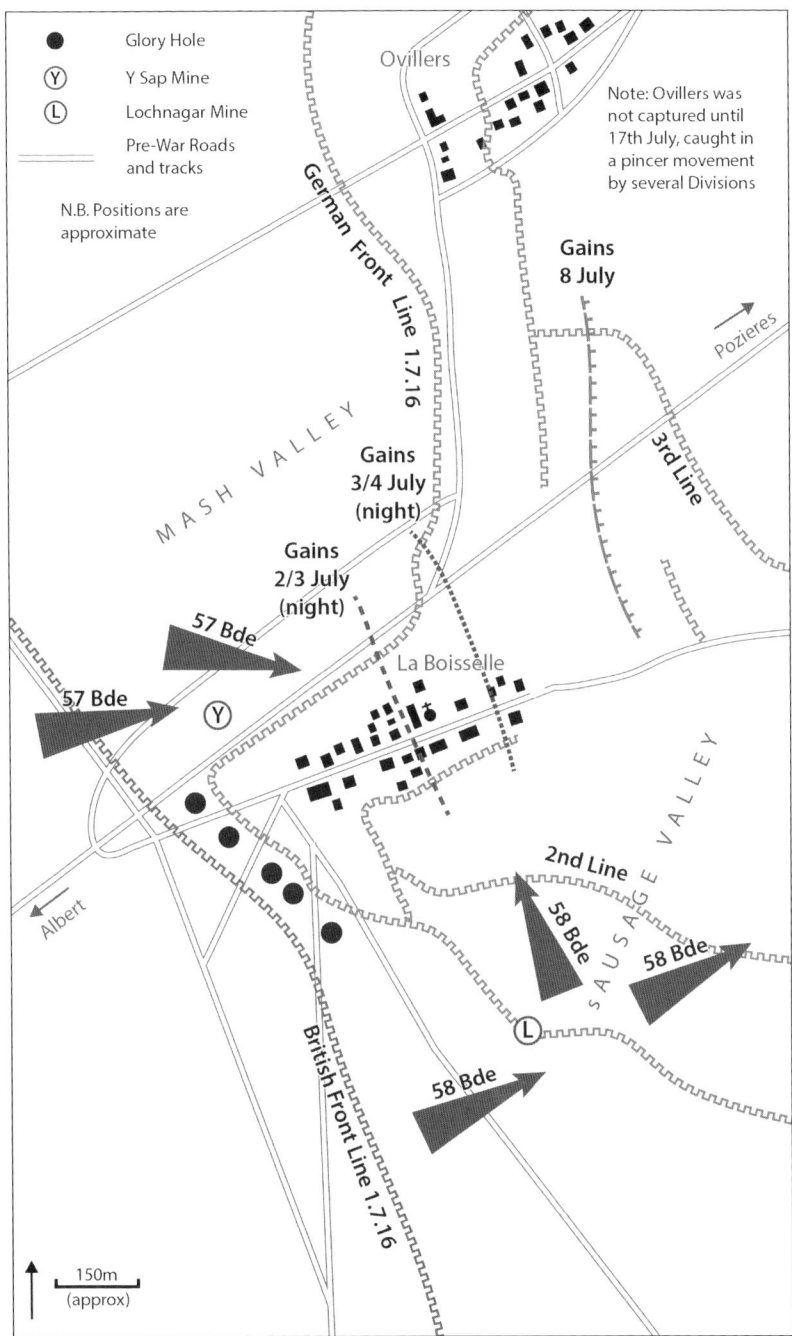

Glory Hole

Y Sap Mine

Lochnagar Mine

Pre-War Roads
and tracks

N.B. Positions are
approximate

Ovillers

Note: Ovillers was
not captured until
17th July, caught in
a pincer movement
by several Divisions

German Front Line 1.7.16

Gains
8 July

Pozieres

3rd Line

MASH VALLEY

Gains
3/4 July
(night)

Gains
2/3 July
(night)

57 Bde

La Boisselle

57 Bde

Y

Albert

2nd Line

58 Bde

58 Bde

L

SAUSAGE VALLEY

58 Bde

British Front Line 1.7.16

150m
(approx)

Figure 8.2 19th Division attacks at La Boisselle.

Figure 8.3 Positions such as this had been flattened by British artillery before the infantry advance. The whereabouts of the deepest dug-outs, however, remained unknown until the village was captured. (Author's collection)

procedures to succeed – rushed across no man's land, storming two lines of trenches before the Germans rallied, sending bombers and close-quarter combatants to meet the threat. The British employed similar tactics, pressing forwards with a grim determination, but by midnight, they had been held up by a well-protected machine-gun post near the church.

Simultaneous counter-attacks pushed the British back, and reserves were sent up at an opportune moment, enabling the momentum to be resumed. In tandem with regiments of other brigades, all but four houses at the eastern edge of the village were secured by the division at around 8 am, yet once again, the Germans were determined to maintain their grip on La Boisselle, launching an intense and sustained assault upon 58 Brigade. By 12:30 pm on 3 July, ground which had been won under such ferocious fire was conceded. In the evening, the 58th was exhausted and badly in need of respite, being finally withdrawn on the 4th.

Remarkably, enemy listening posts and telephone communications in the tip of La Boisselle were still working, enabling the defenders to gain a wider picture of the fighting in their sector, as well as the situation with regard to reinforcements. The Germans had also been ordered to hold on the village under all duress, but their tenure was slowly fading. Unable to rely on artillery support (vital positions nearby had been eliminated by the British), and with promised reserves not materialising when expected, the embattled soldiers were forced to give up crucial areas, including the *Granathof*. Without food or fresh water since the initial attack on 1 July, it is a testament to the resilience of combat soldiers that they held out for so long, and under such extreme conditions. Once they had run out of grenades, the Germans relied upon their deadly machine-guns, knowing that the British were fully committed to storming La Boisselle under any eventuality.

The following officer losses are in battalion order.

Captain Allan Sernberg
9th Battalion, Cheshire Regiment
Killed in action 2 July 1916

Born in Liverpool during 1873, the son of William and Annabella, Allan Sernberg [Figure 8.4] was a career soldier, joining his one and only regiment in 1895. Rising through the ranks, he served in India for several years, and married Martha Rowland in Wales on 5 April 1911. A father of three, he was a company sergeant major by 1913 – "a thoroughly efficient, reliable and hard-working NCO"[3] – and in receipt of a Long Service and Good Conduct Medal. Commissioned from the ranks in December 1914, his thorough grasp of military matters was just what the army needed at this challenging time.

The following and understandably (given the circumstances) confusing testimony, from Private S Holland, of C Company, 9/Cheshires, was dictated from a hospital

---

3   TNA WO339/22015: Capt. A Sernberg service record.

bed in London. Allan Sernberg's officer rank is given as "Major", although he is not described as such in any of the other available records:

> Informant states that on July 2nd 1916, near Albert, as [he] was resting in a big shell hole nick-named 'crater' where he had been for 2 days, it was 'taken' by the Colonel and Lieutenant Hunter and the Major [Sernberg]. Just as the Major was getting out of the shell hole again he got shot in the head and died straight away and was buried at the bottom of the shell hole. Informant thinks he gave this information but as his memory was very bad after lying so long in the shell hole he is not quite certain if he did.[4]

Figure 8.4 Captain A. Sernberg. (Cheshire Regiment Museum)

The length of time Private Holland spent in the 'crater' – the 'Lochnagar' mine, or location of the *Schwaben Höhe* – is open to question. Soldiers of 9/Cheshires were in position near the recently exploded mine by 4:30 am on 2 July, and advanced on La Boisselle just under twelve hours later. It was probably at this time that Captain Sernberg was killed. The crater itself remained in British hands, although the number of wounded men in its immediate environs was disturbingly large (Tyneside Scottish, 10/Lincolns and 11/Suffolks had all suffered heavily at this spot on 1 July), so the retrieval of the injured soldiers was inevitably protracted.

Captain Sernberg, who at the age of forty-three was considerably older than many of his fellow junior officers, has no known grave, and his name is inscribed on the Thiepval Memorial. His death was reported in the 10 July edition of the *Liverpool Echo*, describing him as the 'beloved husband of Martha, of 22 Glengariff Road, Clubmoor'. Rather touchingly for a veteran soldier of over twenty years' experience, he wrote in his will before going overseas to France:

> Everything I have is yours so there should be no trouble. My only regret is that there is not more left for you, but the pension for yourself and the little ones [the youngest had only been born the previous year], in addition to what there is in the Bank, will keep you from want. That is my comfort. Allan.
>
> Goodbye my loves and all.[5]

4   Ibid.
5   Ibid.

Captain Thomas Leslie Jackson, MC
9th Battalion, Cheshire Regiment
Killed in action 2 July 1916

Thomas was a native of Holbeach, Lincolnshire, born in 1893, and his father, Thomas senior, was a medical practitioner, whilst his mother's name was Lucy. The family later moved to Greystoke, near Penrith, in Cumberland (modern Cumbria). Educated at St. Bees Grammar School, south of Whitehaven, and Glasgow University, Thomas Jackson [Figure 8.5] served in the cadet corps and OTC of both educational establishments, although his civilian intention was to become an engineer.

Volunteering in October 1914, his commission soon followed, as did promotion to captain early in 1915. During February 1916, he was awarded the

Figure 8.5 Captain T. Jackson (*Mid Cumberland & Westmorland Herald*)

Military Cross for rescuing a dangerously wounded fellow officer under heavy fire, and close to the enemy lines. Captain Jackson was to have received the medal from the King himself, but pressing matters on the Somme required his presence with the battalion. Lieutenant Colonel RB Morgan informed the officer's parents:

> It is with very deepest sympathy and regret that I have to write and tell you of the death of your son. He died as he lived – splendidly, at the head of his men, who would have followed him everywhere. His loss to you will, I know, be irreparable, as it is to myself and the battalion. He was loved by everyone, and I regarded him as the best officer I had. I have only one consolation to offer, and that is that he was killed instantly by a rifle bullet through the head. I saw him fall myself, so I can vouch for it. He was buried near the spot, and the place marked as well as possible. It is hard to put my feelings into words, but I know that, except his parents, no one could regret his death more than I do.[6]

One of his men, speaking from his hospital bed in Lewisham, stated that early in the day, on 2 July, Captain Jackson had carried out two successful bombing attacks, and at about 7 pm, whilst advancing, the officer was struck down. The 9/Cheshires war diary indicates:

6   *Mid Cumberland & Westmoreland Herald* newspaper, 15 July 1916.

[The battalion] was blocking and clearing out dug-outs [in La Boisselle]. The support line attacked over ground held up by deep and wide communication trenches [whereupon] bombing parties were formed…. Very good work indeed was carried out by Capt. T.L. Jackson (since killed) [and] Lt. C.F. King, who although wounded stuck to it and set a splendid example, only leaving when the position was consolidated.[7]

It can therefore be deduced that Captain Jackson fell within the village of La Boisselle itself. His body was later re-interred at the Gordon Dump Cemetery, several hundred metres from the eastern edge of La Boisselle, and at the head of Sausage Valley.

Inevitably, when researching a large number of individuals, the detailed information available, as well as the possibility of a surviving photograph, varies enormously, and the following is just such an example.

Second Lieutenant Archibald Hunter
13th (attached 9th) Battalion, Cheshire Regiment
Killed in action 2 July 1916

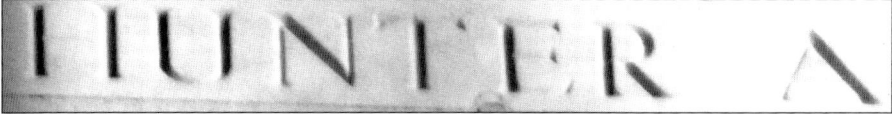

Figure 8.6 Inscription on Thiepval Memorial. (Author's collection)

Archibald was born at Clapham, Surrey in 1875, and his Scottish father Daniel was a licensed victualler at the time, whilst his mother, May, hailed from Hackney. The census returns reveal Archibald's whereabouts every ten years; Rotherhithe, Lambeth and Bloomsbury (1881, 1891 and 1901 respectively), and he started out as a clerk before becoming an estate agent. He married Cecelia in December 1901, and a decade later he was employed as an auctioneer/surveyor, living in Kilburn.

On 6 July 1916, at her home in St George's Road, Mrs Hunter received news that her husband had been killed in action on the 2nd. Private Higgins, of C Company, later reported: 'Informant states that on July 1st [sic], at La Boisselle, he saw his Company Officer, Lt. Hunter, killed in a charge by machine gun fire whilst taking a crater'.[8]

The second lieutenant was mentioned in the recollections of Private Holland, when the latter was asked about the fate of Captain Sernberg, and in addition the war diary alludes to his assistance on the day: 'Lieut. Hunter, Bombing Officer … also gave

---

7   TNA WO95/2090: 9/Cheshires War Diary.
8   TNA WO339/33089: 2/Lt. A Hunter service record.

magnificent aid but was eventually killed'.[9] His name is amongst the many thousands on the Thiepval Memorial [Figure 8.6].

The *Bristol Times and Mirror* revealed on 10 July 1916, that the Germans had 'developed tactics of a disconcerting character, in which they were greatly helped by the swift movements of their machine guns'. (The latter is a reference to the quick assembly of the weapons from their dugouts, when they were able to stem the British advance on 1 July. The 'disconcerting' nature is not all that obvious from a military perspective, unless it is a response to reports of British soldiers being shot in the back once they had passed over hidden enemy strong-points). The narrative then went on to state that the British barrage had 'got them [the enemy] in the neck' and our troops had then 'walked over piles of enemy corpses'. Under the headline of 'Gallant Exploits In The Rain', it specified the work of the Wiltshire Regiment, most probably at La Boisselle on 3 July, as there were several thunderstorms in the area on that day. 'Only one [enemy] officer, and no more than two dead officers, were seen in the field. It is certain that large numbers of Germans have been fighting to a finish without leadership. [We] are not fighting against immature lads and old men. All the men we have fought have been fellows of fine physique'.

[Between 23 June and 3 July, the German regiment holding La Boisselle returned figures of nine officers killed, twelve wounded and a further eight missing.[10] The above newspaper report has obvious propagandist sentiments, but it is entirely possible that members of a single British regiment, for example, may only have seen a handful of enemy officers, dead or alive, during the attack. Fighting in confined trenches, or from behind machine gun nests, contrast the German perspective with that of their British counterparts, who had to advance across exposed ground before the survivors entered the labyrinth in La Boisselle].

6/Wiltshires had fought closely alongside 9/Cheshires on 2–3 July, and so the area of fighting was inevitably similar. Formed in Devizes during September 1914, it understandably attracted a proportion of local men, but there were also a significant number of Londoners both in its officer class, and the rank and file.

Second Lieutenant Arthur Ridley Biggs
6th Battalion, Wiltshire Regiment
Killed in action 2 July 1916

In mid-August 1916, the War Office received the following letter:

> Dear Sir & Cousin.
> May I venture to claim your sympathy to trace a young friend of ours, by name, of 2nd Lieut. Arthur Biggs of the Wiltshire Regt. His relatives fear that he has

9   Ibid.
10 Whitehead, R, *The Other Side Of The Wire Vol II* (Solihull: Helion & Coy., 2013), p. 326.

'gone under' as he has made no sign for 5 or 6 months past, and they can extract no <u>definite</u> information from the Colonel of his unit beyond the fact that he was galantly [sic] leading his platoon near the German trenches at La Boiselle when last seen by his men. The question remains, is he 'dead' or 'alive'? 2nd Lieut. Arthur Biggs got his commission in the Wiltshire Regt. at the commencement of the War after passing through the O.T.C. His people have come to me to help them in their trouble and suspense, and I should be so greatly obliged if you could have a searching enquiry made into the 'Records' at the War Office, and let me know the result.[11]

The communication was signed by Lieutenant Colonel H Storr, of the Middlesex Regiment. A reply came back:

The War Office invariably passes on to the relatives concerned all information in their possession regarding casualties. You can quite understand that, in an advance, it is impossible for officers or men to note exactly what happens to their comrades. Their business is to devote themselves entirely to the attack and the work in hand, and not attending to the wounded or tracing the missing.[12]

Born on 14 October 1893, at Lower Edmonton in Middlesex, Arthur Biggs was the son of James and Ellen. By 1911 he was living with his family in Itchen, Hampshire, and training to become a teacher. He also attended Reading University [Figure 8.7] before receiving his commission in December 1914. Although 6/Wiltshires arrived in France with the rest of the 19th Division during July 1915, Second Lieutenant Biggs' medal index card reveals he did not join them in France until 22 April 1916, when the battalion was stationed at Robecq, near Bethune. Over the following weeks, all ranks were engaged in preparations for

Figure 8.7 Second Lieutenant A.R. Biggs. (Reading University)

11   TNA WO339/28564: 2/Lt. AR Biggs service record.
12   Ibid.

the forthcoming attack, with the war diary of 15 May revealing: 'Platoon training – special importance being given to Platoon Commanders. Attacking and consolidating trenches, night bombing and Parish wiring'.[13]

The same diary on 2 July does not reveal much information other than the battalion advanced in open order at 4 pm and attacked the German front line system just south of La Boisselle. Two lines of trenches were taken and consolidated, but casualties had been heavy. One of the officers later reported 'missing' was Second Lieutenant Biggs, whose father made every effort possible to discover the fate of his son: 'From letters received from the front, and from enquiries made from the wounded in hospitals in this country, we [are] fearing that he had been killed in the attack of July 2nd near Boisselle'.[14]

The War Office then sent a reply to Arthur Biggs, informing him that his worst fears had been realised following confirmation from the commanding officer of 6/Wiltshires, who stated Second Lieutenant Biggs had, indeed, fallen at La Boisselle. The officer lies buried at Ovillers Military Cemetery [Figure 8.8]. The graves face the houses and northern ridge of La Boisselle, looking across Mash Valley.

Figure 8.8 Ovillers Military Cemetery. (Author's collection)

13   TNA WO95/2093: 6/Wiltshires War Diary.
14   TNA WO339/28564: 2/Lt. AR Biggs service record.

Second Lieutenant Lawrence John Maynard Allen
6th Battalion, Wiltshire Regiment
Killed in action 2 July 1916

Figure 8.9 Second Lieutenant L.J.M. Allen. (Pam & Ken Linge)

Born towards the end of 1896 in the Brixton area of South London, Lawrence was the son of Henry – a teacher at a special school – and Jane. He attended Emmanuel School in nearby Battersea, where he served in the Officer Training Corps, and he enlisted as a private into 2/London Regiment (the City of London battalion of the Royal Fusiliers) in October 1914, serving in Malta until the following August. Commissioned into the Wiltshire Regiment, Second Lieutenant Allen [Figure 8.9] arrived in France on Christmas Day 1915, when the 6th Battalion was holding the trenches near Bethune. Although the enemy was described as 'quiet' by the war diary, Company Quarter Master Sergeant Merritt was killed by a 'whizz-bang' (an artillery shell from a German field gun) on this date.

After the attack in early July 1916, Second Lieutenant BP Springette, who was wounded during the advance, told a board of enquiry: 'I saw Lt. Maynard [he meant Second Lieutenant Allen, whose second middle name was Maynard] killed on 2nd July at La Boisselle. He was killed straight off'.[15]

Private J Moore, of C Company, who was also injured and in hospital, stated that as they were attacking the German trenches: 'I saw Lt. Allen fall wounded in the head – in all probability killed'.[16] It would seem the officer had fallen whilst advancing towards La Boisselle from the area of the new crater sometime after 4 pm. He is remembered at Thiepval, so it is clear that his body (if recovered at all) was not identifiable. (One of the many grim facts about the First World War was that corpses could be subjected to the ravages of future shell-fire and explosions, thus rendering them unrecognisable as even human remains).

Second Lieutenant Allen's family were informed via a telegram that the officer had 'died of wounds received in action',[17] although it seems unlikely he received treatment at a medical facility before his death, as he would almost certainly have then been buried in a marked grave. He was still a teenager when he met his demise.

15   TNA WO339/43215: 2/Lt. LJM Allen service record.
16   Ibid.
17   Ibid.

Second Lieutenant John Maurice Hunter
6th Battalion, Wiltshire Regiment
Killed in action 2 July 1916

If ever there was an example of intellect, athleticism and promise cut short by the Great War, it can be found in the story of John Hunter. Born on 17 April 1885, he was the eldest son of Rev Dr John Hunter, and he was educated at Glasgow's Kelvinside Acadamy, University College School, London, and finally Baillol College, Oxford. At the latter seat of learning he obtained a second class in modern history, and became secretary and vice president of the Arnold Society, which was famous for its lively debates. (The Prime Minister between 1908 and 1916, Herbert Asquith, was a former

Figure 8.10 Second Lieutenant J. Hunter. (Author's collection)

Baillol student, as was his son, Raymond, who fell in action at Flers whilst serving as a lieutenant in the Grenadier Guards. Asquith junior was older than John Hunter, but their paths may have crossed at alumni gatherings before the conflict).

John Hunter [Figure 8.10] was a fine sportsman and tennis player, as well as becoming a proficient climber and budding playwright. He worked in a publishing house, then as a journalist, and finally at the Board of Education, relinquishing the latter appointment upon joining the army. He proceeded to the front in October 1915, and several months later he was appointed the battalion grenadier, or bombing, officer. His father, who was formerly a minister at the Trinity Congregational Church in Glasgow, later lived in London's Hampstead district.

After the attack on La Boisselle, Second Lieutenant Hunter's commanding officer wrote: 'How much we all feel the loss of your son. He was one of the bravest men I ever met, and he died carrying out a most difficult task, displaying the greatest gallantry possible. I regret his loss not only as an asset to the English army but as a personal friend'. (It was noted that the task to which the CO was referring to had been undertaken 'voluntarily'). Second Lieutenant Hunter's captain added: 'He was a great favourite. He died fighting splendidly, doing great work'. His sergeant, who was at the officer's side when he fell, concluded: 'His dash and fearlessness, together with his remarkable courage, put new life into the men at an anxious moment'.[18]

---

18   *Bristol Times & Mirror* newspaper, 13 July 1916.

From the tone of these reports, it seems likely Second Lieutenant Hunter was killed during the fierce close-quarter fighting within the trenches of La Boisselle, when the Germans deployed their own bombers to counter the British advance. His body is believed to be buried in the Gordon Dump Cemetery, close to that of Captain Thomas Jackson, MC, of 9/Cheshires.

Second Lieutenant Edmund Harold King
6th Battalion, Wiltshire Regiment
Died of wounds 3 July 1916

Rather strangely, Edmund King has two places of birth noted on his service record – St Mark's, Reigate, Surrey, and South Holme, Sylvan Road, Upper Norwood. The latter was given by his mother, Jessie, so it can be taken as correct. Born on 17 October 1889, Edmund and his family were living at the Sylvan Road address two years later, where William, the head of the household, was employed as an army and navy equipment contractor. Ten years on, Edmund was a boarder at St Aubyn's School, Eastbourne, and he later became a scholar at Queen's College, Cambridge. When he joined the army (his commission was confirmed in the *London Gazette* in early January 1915) he gave his occupation as 'student at Cambridge University'.[19] Beyond this brief synopsis, little more is known about him. Second Lieutenant Springett[e], who witnessed the death of Second Lieutenant Allen, reported that he had seen Second Lieutenant King 'dying of his wounds at La Boiselle. He died 30 minutes after being seen* at 8 p.m. [on 2 July]'.[20] If this was the case, then the date of death in the official records is incorrect, although the location of his grave – at the Heilly Station Cemetery, Mericourt L'Abbe (several miles to the south-west of Albert) would tally with him dying on 3 July, as it may have taken several hours to transport him overnight from the congested battlefield to 36 Casualty Clearing Station, which had been located at Heilly since April 1916. [*The eye-witness does not confirm precisely where he had seen Second Lieutenant King shortly before the officer died].

The *Wiltshire Telegraph* noted on 8 July 1916: 'So far only one name of a Wiltshire Regiment officer has been mentioned, officially or unofficially, as killed or wounded in the last week. It occurs this morning, and is that of Second Lieutenant Harold King, who died of wounds on July 3rd. He was 27 years old, and was the younger son of the late Mr. W. King, and of Mrs. King, of Reigate'. (The *Wiltshire Gazette* also carried a short obituary, which contained the same information. The newspaper was distributed in Devizes, and as the 6th Battalion originated from here, it is likely this was the only connection the officer had with the town).

The *War List of the University of Cambridge 1914-1919* (edited by GV Carey, MA) contains a discrepancy. The only 'EH King' listed is a second lieutenant in the Royal

---

19   TNA WO339/82379: 2/Lt. EH King service record.
20   Ibid.

Sussex Regiment, killed in action in July *1917*. No such officer with this exact name died whilst serving with the Royal Sussex Regiment, so this is most probably a clerical error, and should refer instead to Second Lieutenant EH King of the Wiltshires.

With Second Lieutenant King's final hours in mind, it is prudent to focus upon the procedures which had been arranged for the treatment and evacuation of the wounded during the Somme offensive. Few could have predicted the sheer scale of bloodshed which took place, and the medical teams were literally overwhelmed by the colossal numbers which poured through the system. (In mid-June, however, General Rawlinson had made contingencies for the processing of 10,000 injured troops *per day*,[21] just as a precaution). A stricken soldier's first port of call was the regimental aid post, normally situated close to, or within, the front line trenches, and for those with slight wounds, the attention they received here may sometimes have proved sufficient for a swift return to duty. But by the very nature of crossing no man's land under heavy fire, and (for those who managed to progress further) the subsequent hand-to-hand fighting in the enemy positions, the threat to life and limb was clearly much more acute.

Advanced dressing stations, field ambulances and casualty clearing stations each provided more thorough degrees of medical expertise, and the cases which were 'sitting' or 'lying' (i.e. those usually brought in by stretcher bearers, or with the assistance of comrades) were assessed according to the severity of their injuries. Motor lorries and ambulance trains were also at the disposal of the authorities, taking the battle-scarred men to base hospitals closer to the French coast with a view to eventually bringing them back to 'Blighty' itself. Inevitably, the retrieval of the wounded closest to the German positions which were still swept by machine-guns and snipers proved to be the most dangerous of tasks, and undoubtedly many perished who would otherwise have lived had they received even rudimentary care from those trained to deal with such eventualities. (58 Brigade's war diary, for example, noted that on 2 July, the German line near the new crater, which had just been reached by 9/Cheshires, was found to be full of British wounded '… lying in it fairly thickly').[22] The cemeteries which sprang up close to casualty clearing stations, such as the one at Heilly, were an all too abundant consequence of those unfortunates who did not live long enough to proceed down the carefully planned evacuation chain.

At 11 am on 2 July, the war diary of 59 Field Ambulance, part of the 19th Division's medical team, recorded: 'Wire received to expand accommodation to utmost capacity. All tents pitched and adjacent barns prepared for the reception of the wounded'.[23]

Its sister unit, 57 FA, noted on the same day: 'Received orders…that [Stretcher] Bearer Division would be required to proceed to assembly trenches SW of Albert.

21   Middlebrook, M, *The First Day On The Somme – 1 July 1916* (London: Penguin 1984), p. 84.
22   TNA WO95/2087: 58 Brigade HQ War Diary.
23   TNA WO95/2073/1: 59 Field Ambulance War Diary.

Figure 8.11 German prisoners and British escorts make their way back from
the fierce fighting at La Boisselle. (Private collection)

466 cases admitted to Field Ambulance before noon and have all been evacuated by
motor lorries. 700 cases have been detained and evacuated by lorries. Total – 1166'.[24]

By 4 July, 2028 men had been processed, and the position was targeted by German
shelling on the 6th, killing one of the medics and injuring eight more. Nine wounded
officers were brought in during the night, one of whom later died. Forty-seven men in
the ranks were also admitted, 'nearly all were very serious cases'.[25]

The war diary for 9/Royal Welch Fusiliers[26] notes on 2 July that the assaulting
battalions 'gained considerable ground towards their objective before darkness set in',
and praise was awarded to the company commanders who led their men across no man's
land with 'great skill'. The subsequent bombing duel in the trenches came at 'considerable cost', whilst counter-attacks by the enemy 'in co-operation with his snipers, who
proved to be very deadly' were launched. The latter, hidden in ruined houses, also
caused significant casualties throughout the day on the 3rd, and the German advance
which pushed the British back was 'rigorously sustained' until checked. A block was
established which kept the bombers at bay, and in the evening, another assault was

24   TNA WO95/2072/1: 57 Field Ambulance War Diary.
25   Ibid.
26   TNA WO95/2092: 9/Royal Welch Fusiliers War Diary.

thwarted by a 'hastily constructed parados and traverse'. The Fusiliers were withdrawn at 2:00 am on the 4th, still harassed by sharp-shooters and grenadiers close by.

The battalion had been raised in Wrexham during September 1914, and the following officer casualties are in order of their believed date of death, rather than their superiority of rank. With such large scale losses in the opening days of July 1916, it was impossible to accurately pin-point the time and or even sometimes the day a particular officer lost his life. (The spelling of 'Welch' in the RWF is a nod to the origins of the regiment, founded in 1689. It is also, of course, written as 'Welsh').

Captain Ernest Kerrison Jones
8th (attached 9th) Battalion, Royal Welch Fusiliers
Killed in action 2–3 July 1916

'The sympathy of the townspeople at large will go out to Mr and Mrs J Kerrison Jones, Glasfryn, Wrexham, in the sad loss which they have suffered by the death in action of their second son, Capt. Ernest Jones. The sad event took place on Sunday week [2 July] …'.[27]

Born in Wrexham on 16 April 1892, Ernest was the son of John – the corporate borough collector – and Annie. He secured the Mayor's Gold Medal, which was offered annually in connection with Wrexham County School, and he later studied mathematics at University College, Oxford [Figure 8.12], where he was also a member of the OTC. '[He] had a brilliant scholastic career, and was undoubtedly destined for a high posi-

Figure 8.12 Captain E.K. Jones. (University College, Oxford)

tion in civil life had his patriotism not been greater than all other considerations'.[28] Just days after the outbreak of war, he joined 8/RWF (which became part of the 13th Division), a unit raised in Wrexham, so this was very much his local regiment. Second Lieutenant Jones served in Gallipoli during 1915, one of the few officers of the 19th Division to see active service away from the Western Front, and during this time he was slightly wounded, as well as contracting dysentery, hepatitis and jaundice. Invalided home for a time, having attained the rank of captain, he was then

27 *North Wales Guardian* newspaper, 14 July 1916.
28 Ibid.

transferred to 9/RWF in France, whose commanding officer, Colonel RA Berners, had the sombre duty of writing to the officer's father in July 1916:

> I deeply regret having to tell you of the death of your son, who was killed while commanding A Company of my battalion in the recent fighting. On Saturday (1st July) we were called upon to assault the German trenches opposing us, near the village of La Boisselle (near Albert). This involved a charge over 150 yards of ground swept by machine guns. This was gallantly carried out by the battalion, and it was shortly after gaining the German lines that your son was killed... I have lost the assistance of an officer of considerable ability and promise. In this fighting, the brigade [58] has earned the praise of the 1st Army Commander [he may have been referring to General Rawlinson, the *Fourth* Army Commander], but the success earned is due almost entirely to the young men who, like your son, have come forward and trained and led the men so splendidly.[29]

Captain Jones' parents received a telegram on 6 July 1916, informing them their son had been killed on the 2nd. The Commonwealth War Graves Commission also agrees with the date, and it is only the *Officers Died in The Great War* relating to the Royal Welch Fusiliers which states it was on the 3rd. The war diary also tallies with the former, and lists the death of Captain Jones after the mention of the enemy snipers in La Boisselle who had proved to be 'very deadly'.

Aged 24, Captain Jones is remembered at Thiepval. 'It is perhaps only natural that he should [have] immediately offered his services to his country in its hour of need'.[30]

Second Lieutenant Charles Duncan McCammon
9th Battalion, Royal Welch Fusiliers
Killed in action 2–3 July 1916

Charles McCammon began his army career in the ranks of 6/Royal Inniskilling Fusiliers, which had been formed in Omagh, Northern Ireland, in August 1914, before receiving his commission in 9/RWF. He subsequently arrived in France during early October 1915. He was the son of Andrew and Madeline McCammon, born on 25 March 1892, at Seaforde, County Down, and prior to the war he was a clerk at

Figure 8.13 Second Lieutenant C.D. McCammon. (Campbell College, Belfast)

29 Ibid.
30 Ibid.

the Ulster Bank. His education took place at Campbell College, Belfast [Figure 8.13] and Coleraine Academical Institution.

There is no report of his death, either in his service record or local newspaper. (The latter – the *Newtownard Chronicle and County Down Observer* – revealed in mid-July the officer had been killed on the 2nd of that month, but erroneously gave his age as twenty, not twenty-four). Unlike Captain Ernest Jones, Second Lieutenant McCammon has a marked grave, which is situated in Ovillers Military Cemetery.

The following officer came from a family steeped in Welsh history, and is one which draws upon many of the facets for which the Great War has become renowned: duty, despair, sacrifice, honour and abiding camaraderie.

Lieutenant Cadwalader Glyn Roberts
9th Battalion, Royal Welch Fusiliers
Killed in action 3 July 1916

Figure 8.14 Lieutenant C.G. Roberts.
(Bangor University)

There is a poignant moment (one of a number, of course) in Wyn Griffith's memoir *Up To Mametz*, when the author, a captain in 15/RWF, describes his wartime experiences, most notably with the 38th (Welsh) Division at Mametz Wood in July 1916, a few short miles from La Boisselle, and only a matter of days after the exploits of the 19th Division. Captain Griffith, who was a contemporary of famous war poets and authors such as Siegfried Sassoon, Robert Graves and Ellis Evans (the latter also known by his literary *pseudonym* 'Hedd Wyn'), encountered the brigade signal officer – whom he calls 'Taylor' in the book, although the correct identity was Captain Emlyn H Davies – on 7 July, and the latter relayed a story when he had met 'old Evans, the padre' early that morning. Davies was concerned about the minister's appearance and demeanour, as he was talking to himself 'in North Wales Welsh', and mentioned he hadn't been to bed at all the previous night because he had been looking for the grave of a recently fallen soldier – that of his own son, 'killed near Fricourt the day before'. It was, in fact, four days earlier. He had walked in vain for hours, unable to find anyone who knew where his boy was buried, so he had come back to Mametz Wood to bury other lads, and pray over their final resting places.

Captain Davies tried to converse with the padre in Welsh, as he felt it was inappropriate to speak in English at a time like that. He remembered: 'There was some shrapnel overhead, but I saw him going up the slope as if he were alone in the world'.[31] After much research, Pat Evans, of the Western Front Association, uncovered the true identity of 'old Evans, the padre' – the Rev Peter Jones Roberts, a Wesleyan Methodist minister originally from Barmouth, a coastal town in north Wales. (Wyn Griffith changed the names of several individuals in the book). Rev Roberts' son, Cadwalader (known as Glyn) was born on 31 August 1894, and attended Kingswood Scool in Bath, and Friars School, Bangor, before winning the John Hughes Scholarship at the University of North Wales, in the same location. [Figure 8.14]. He was a student here from October 1912 until the summer of 1914, reading Latin and French. Commissioned into 9/RWF shortly after war broke out, he arrived in France during July 1915, and went home on leave just six weeks prior to the Somme offensive.

His father, meanwhile, was also eager to do his bit, applying to become an army chaplain at the front, but his age – fifty-one in 1914 – went against him. Undaunted, he persevered, lobbying senior church men and politicians until his wish was granted. At the French port of Le Havre, where many soldiers disembarked, he helped to set up a rest and entertainment hut for those passing through, yet he felt that even this was not his true vocation, and finally he was attached to the 38th (Welsh) Division, where he accompanied the men into the forward lines, as well as offering his services at various casualty clearing stations. He was popular and selfless, gaining widespread respect for his often difficult mission in the combat zone as he tried to represent humanity and calm amongst the carnage.

On 2 July 1916, the war diary for 9/RWF mentions the enemy snipers causing severe casualties from their positions in ruined houses, adding: '2/Lt. Wancke, [the] Battalion Signal Officer, was wounded, [and] Lt. CG Roberts, Adjutant, was killed as he ran to his assistance'.[32] The officer was also described as: '… a youth of more than ordinary intellectual ability, frank and lovable in disposition, and of sterling character'.[33]

It is something of a sad irony that Lieutenant Roberts is *believed* to be buried at Ovillers Military Cemetery, and his name is on one of the special memorials there, so his grieving father may never have seen the grave he so desperately sought anyway. (His three other sons all served with the Royal Welch Fusiliers, and all survived, although one was posted 'missing' before being declared a prisoner of war, another was badly wounded, and the third received a Military Cross for gallantry. Rev Roberts returned home after the conflict, physically and mentally shattered by the ordeal. In June 1921, he went out sea fishing on his own near Bangor, and never returned. His body was found caught in a fishing net in the Menai Straits with his watch stopped at 1:10 pm).

31   Griffith, LW, (Editor: Riley, J) *Up to Mametz…And Beyond* (Barnsley: Pen & Sword, 2010), pp. 98–99.
32   TNA WO95/2092: 9/Royal Welch Fusiliers War Diary.
33   Bangor University Archives.

The University of Bangor recorded in Welsh that '….in the great battle with the Prussian Guards at a place called La Boiselle, [Lieutenant CG Roberts] fell in battle on July 3rd 1916, aged 21 years'.[34] In deference to his father's grief at Pommiers Redoubt, near Mametz, when he encountered Captain Emlyn Davies, the following epitaph remains in his native tongue:

Yr Arglwydd yw fy Mugail,
O! fendigedig ffaith,
Cynhyrcha wir orfoledd
I'm henaid ar fy nhaith[35]

The fourth regiment of 58 Brigade, 9/Welsh, was in support of the other three battalions, although its bombers were attached to 9/RWF. D Company had been detailed to dig a communication trench from the old British front line towards La Boisselle, but this was only rendered possible after dark due to hostile machine gun fire. A and B Companies carried grenades and small arms ammunition across no man's land during the assault, and then assisted in the capture of the village itself. Consolidation and extending newly captured lines continued until the men were withdrawn on 4 July, in preparation for a new attack several days later.

Lieutenant Oswald Robert John Green
9th Battalion, Welsh Regiment
Died of wounds 5 July 1916

Born in Aberystwyth, central Wales, on 24 January 1881, he was the son of William – an engineer at the local foundry – and Sophia. He grew up in the town, attending Jasper House School, followed by the University College of Wales (in the same location), where he belonged to the College Volunteers. In addition, he was at one time in the Cardigan Battery, a Territorial branch of the artillery. A renowned sportsman, Oswald [Figure 8.15] excelled at swimming, cricket ('a proficient bowler and hard hitter for the Ceredigion Club'),[36] golf, and most

Figure 8.15 Lieutenant O.R.J. Green.
(*The Cambrian News*)

34   Ibid.
35   Ibid. A translation into English did not seem appropriate.
36   *The Cambrian News & Welsh Farmers' Gazette* newspaper, 14 July 1916.

notably football, appointed captain of Aberystwyth FC and guiding the club to one of its most successful seasons in the cup and league during the early years of the 20th Century. Several English teams tried to persuade him to turn professional, but he declined, and one of his strengths lay in his protection of his fellow players if any of them was tackled heavily or fouled by an opponent.

Living and working as an engineer in the United States when war broke out, he returned home as 1914 drew to a close and was given a commission in the Welsh Regiment. He had married Winifred during 1906, and just months before sailing back to Wales he had become a father to Joan. He was also the holder of a Royal Humane Society Medal for saving the life of an individual who was drowning.

There is no indication of how Lieutenant Green received his fatal injuries during the assault, and the only definitive information came from the officer commanding 38 casualty clearing station at Heilly, to the south-west of Albert, where the stricken officer was brought and subsequently 'died of wounds received in action'.[37] The Welshman's body was then buried at the Heilly Station Cemetery, one of nearly 3,000 British and Commonwealth servicemen interred here. Lieutenant Green was aged 35 at the time of his demise, and his wife received a telegram days later informing her of his death.

German accounts of the fighting in La Boisselle on 2 July tell of desperate struggles, exhaustion, battle fatigue and mounting casualties. It is to be remembered that they had successfully stalled the attack of the 34th Division the previous day, and were now tasked with repelling a British onslaught launched by fresh troops. The lack of water, medical assistance and new reserves of their own were already proving critical to the defenders, but they still grimly fought on. The explosion of the two mines had inevitably caused significant death and injury, and the salient was now being targeted from both sides. Although reinforced with a handful of men who managed to reach the village under fire, the overwhelming numbers of enemy soldiers who were then seen advancing towards them must have signalled to the Germans their fate was finally sealed.

At around 8:30 pm on 2 July, an incident is recorded which details the death of a British officer from a German perspective. Severely weakened by almost constant combat, many of the defending companies holding the outer reaches of La Boisselle were finally pushed back, whereupon *Offizier Aspirant* Brachat ordered his men out from one of the underground shelters and into the fray, only to be wounded by a hand grenade which set the dugout on fire. As Brachat climbed the steps to escape over the bodies of his fallen comrades, an officer in khaki raised his pistol at him but was immediately shot dead by a German named Forster. At that moment, many British soldiers swarmed through and took Brachat prisoner.

---

37   TNA WO339/22314: Lt. ORJ Green service record.

Figure 8.16 German trenches prior to an attack. Note the rifles placed in readiness should the alarm sound. (Author's collection)

It is impossible to pin-point exactly who the officer was, but he almost certainly belonged to 58 Brigade, and from the known testimonies of two of the individuals mentioned in this chapter, I believe it was either Captain Thomas Jackson, MC, 9/Cheshires, who was seen by his CO shot through the head with a rifle bullet whilst engaged in bombing attacks in the communication trenches, or Second Lieutenant John Hunter, 6/Wiltshires, who fell gallantly leading his men and putting new life into them at an anxious moment. Whoever it was, he possessed immense courage, knowing that death lurked around every corner.

In comparison to the other battalions around them, 9/Welsh suffered relatively few casualties during the attack on La Boisselle itself, but on 6 July, its men were sent back to the front line, this time situated to the south-east of the village, facing Sausage Valley. Their objective was Heligoland Trench, near Contalmaison [see Figure 10.6], and attached to the unit at this time were the bombers from 5/South Wales Borderers, the 19th Division's Pioneers, under Lieutenant Clarence Hall, MC. At 8:15 am on the 7th, leading platoons crept over the parapet, whilst others made their way along communication trenches. Orders had been issued to keep behind the creeping barrage – a British artillery bombardment timed to target a portion of the German defences before moving on to the next one, allowing the infantry to keep pace under its supposed protection – although some of the soldiers went forward too quickly and were caught under its deadly work. Two companies of 9/Welsh veered off course into Contalmaison, teaming up with soldiers of the neighbouring 23rd Division, but the entire operation in the area around Bailiff Wood caused every officer of the battalion to become a casualty, killed, wounded or missing.

Trench systems were captured, however, as were around 400 prisoners, with the assistance of 6/Wiltshires, 9/RWF, and 9/Cheshires. During the afternoon, German snipers caused many problems as the lines were consolidated, and bombing parties were dispatched to negate the threat. 'The state of the battered trenches was appalling and any movement along them was necessarily very hard work and slow',[38] noted 9/Cheshires' war diary. All ranks had to endure the attentions of high explosive and gas shells, and on the 8th, a potential counter-attack from the direction of Contalmaison (which was still in German hands) was thwarted by a British artillery strike. 9/Welsh returned to billets the following day.

---

38   TNA WO95/2090: 9/Cheshires War Diary.

Figure 8.17 The flat, open and featureless landscape to the south-east of La Boisselle. This image is looking north-eastwards from the British front line of 1 July 1916. To the left (and unseen) is the Lochnagar Crater and then La Boisselle itself. To the right of the trees on the horizon (and also unseen) is the village of Contalmaison. (Author's collection)

Second Lieutenant Reginald Charles Cooke, MC
9th Battalion, Welsh Regiment
Killed in action 7 July 1916

Figure 8.18 Second Lieutenant R.C. Cooke MC. (Pam & Ken Linge)

A native of Roath, Cardiff, born on 17 June 1886, his father, Charles, was a grocer, and his mother's name was Annie. He grew up in the Welsh capital before moving to Weston-super-mare in Somerset, where he became a solicitor in 1911. His chosen sport was hockey, representing the Weston XI, Somerset and West, and as an international with Wales. Just before the outbreak of war, Reginald [Figure 8.18] accepted a partnership in a south Wales legal firm, back in Cardiff, but set aside his civilian career when he enlisted as a private in 11/Welsh Regiment. Commissioned as a second lieutenant in the 9th battalion during 1915, he was twice mentioned in dispatches as well as receiving a Military Cross for repeated acts of bravery.

After the engagement at Bailiff Wood on 7 July 1916, Second Lieutenant Cooke was reported as 'missing believed killed'. The *Weston-super-Mare Gazette* later revealed:

> The official notification….held out a faint hope that he might still be alive, but now, unfortunately, that slender hope has been ruthlessly destroyed. Letters have been received by the bereaved family of the promising young officer, which,

while bearing testimony to his sterling work, give some details which leave no doubt as to his fate. The Colonel of the regiment, and also a brother officer, have written [to them] from which it appears that in the attack 2/Lt. Cooke's platoon had to retire, the officers being all killed or wounded. The Colonel ascertained from the men who were with Lieut. Cooke that he was shot through the head. His orderly, who also went back to search for him, never returned ...[39]

Second Lieutenant CH Golding (most probably the 'brother officer' mentioned above) also stated he saw Lieutenant Cooke 'shot in the head in a German trench on 7 July',[40] but could not report it until later because he had been wounded himself. Thirty year old Second Lieutenant Reginald Cooke, MC, is commemorated at Thiepval.

Second Lieutenant Godfrey Gwilyn Brychan Stephens
9th Battalion, South Wales Borderers (attached 9th Battalion, Welsh Regiment)
Killed in action 7 July 1916

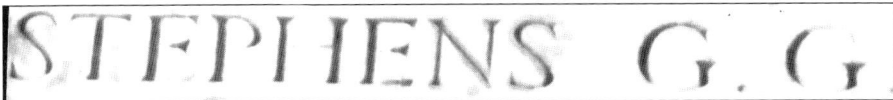

Figure 8.19 Inscription on Thiepval Memorial. (Author's collection)

Although born at Wellingborough, Northamptonshire, on 28 April 1895, Godfrey had strong Welsh roots. His father, Thomas, was a Congregational minister, originally from Brecon, as was Anne, Godfrey's mother (the couple were married in their home town during 1886). A new pastoral role for Rev Stephens brought the family firstly to Camberwell in South London, followed by a parish in New Malden, Surrey. Godfrey was working as a clerk when he joined the 9th County of London Regiment (Queen Victoria's Rifles) as a private in August 1914, and he went to France with his battalion in early November. His desire to serve in 'any Welsh regiment'[41] was granted in March 1915, when he was commissioned into the South Wales Borderers. (The previous month he had been invalided home with frost-bite).

He was initially attached to 3/Welsh Regiment, a Cardiff based reserve unit, before being transferred to the 9th. On 7 July 1916, the war diary lists Second Lieutenant Stephens as 'killed', although no other detail exists. His death was reported in the *Wimbledon Borough News* several weeks later, revealing the twenty-one year old was the second son of the late Rev Thomas Stephens, BA, FRGS. (The young officer had made a will on 26 June 1916, leaving everything to his mother).

39 *Weston-super-mare Gazette* newspaper, 22 July 1916.
40 TNA WO339/40345: 2/Lt. RC Cooke service record.
41 TNA WO339/5848: 2/Lt. GGB Stephens service record.

Compared with the congested nature of the fighting within La Boisselle, it is far more difficult to find the exact location of a particular individual's death out on the open battlefield, where the fortunes swung to and fro over a fairly wide area. The officer is also remembered at Thiepval [Figure 8.19 – author's collection].

Temporary Lieutenant Ivor Guest Rees
9th Battalion, Welsh Regiment
Died of wounds 5 August 1916

In mid-July 1916, the *Llanelly Star* announced under the headline 'Wounded but Cheerful':

> The news was received on Thursday that a young Llanelly officer, Lieut. Ivor Rees, who belongs to one of the Welsh Regiments, had been wounded, and that he is missing. Lieut. Rees, prior to the war, was on the clerical staff at the Old Castle Tinplate Works. Yesterday, we are glad to say, a further message came to hand that Lieut. Rees was not missing. He was wounded in the shoulder and was quite cheerful.[42]

Born at Llanelly (the spelling is correct as of the time period), west Wales, on 21 September 1892, Ivor was the son of William, an engineer, and Annie, and a member of an esteemed Carmarthenshire family. (Two of his uncles were an alderman, and a divisional superintendent of the Great Western Railway, respectively). Educated at the local county school, he was admitted in January 1907, and when he left, he gave his proposed employment as 'clerk' (at the nearby foundry).

Ivor joined the ranks of the King's Shropshire Light Infantry in 1914, and received his officer's commission the following year. The *Llanelly Star* also revealed that he had become a soldier of 'high spirit and splendid gallantry'. Once again, his final movements in the attack at Bailiff Wood are not forthcoming, although his service record[43] notes he was admitted to Number 2 Red Cross Hospital, Rouen (on the French coast) suffering from 'GSW [gunshot wound] head', whilst its nature was deemed to be 'slight'. However, septic poisoning set in, rendering him weaker by the day, until his mother made the long journey from Wales to be at his side. At 12:40 am on 5 August, Lieutenant Rees succumbed to his injuries, and his body was buried in the Officers' Section at the nearby St. Sever Cemetery. He was aged twenty-three. (His brother, Vivian, died in the United Kingdom during May 1918, whilst serving with 7/Welsh Regiment).

---

42   *Llanelly Star* newspaper, 10 August 1916.
43   TNA WO339/27472: Lt IG Rees service record.

Figure 8.20 Trenches dug into the chalk close to a wood shattered by artillery shells.
(Author's collection)

The Welsh theme in 58 Brigade continues with 5/South Wales Borderers, the Pioneers of the 19th Division mentioned earlier. Formed at Brecon in September 1914, the battalion arrived in France the following July, and a year later, on 1 July 1916, it assisted the survivors of the doomed 8th Division, which attacked Ovillers across Mash Valley, by bringing in the wounded during the evening, with several of its men distinguishing themselves in the rescue. Over the next few days it was employed in digging communication trenches towards La Boisselle, as the village gradually fell into British hands, and after a brief respite, returned to assist 58 Brigade on 6 July, being attached to 9/Welsh. Companies were engaged as carrying parties, transporting water, bombs and stores up to the front line. Meanwhile, its bombing section had accompanied the infantry into the assault, resulting in the loss of one of its officers.

Lieutenant Clarence Espeut Lyon Hall, MC
5th Battalion, South Wales Borderers
Killed in action 7 July 1916

Born on 16 February 1896, Clarence was the son
of Clarence senior and Noemi [as spelt by the
CWGC]. The family had links with Jamaica,
where his parents were living after the war,
although during the conflict, the officer's father
had an address in London's Kensington. Clarence
junior enlisted into 9/London Regiment in
September 1914, from his home in Chiswick.
He had already served with the Oundle OTC
in Northamptonshire, and just a month after
joining the army, he was a second lieutenant,
becoming a full lieutenant exactly a year later.
His service record[44] reveals he was wounded
in action in late December 1915, but remained
at duty, and the announcement of his Military
Cross was published in the *London Gazette*
during June 1916.

Figure 8.21 Lieutenant C.E.L.
Hall (RWF Museum)

The circumstances of his death are not to hand. His body lies buried at the Becourt
Military Cemetery, Becordel-Becourt, between Albert and Fricourt. Aged twenty
when he fell, [Figure 8.21 and Figure 8.22] both of the photographs are reprinted
courtesy of the Regimental Museum of the Royal Welsh.

Figure
8.22 Lt. C.E.L.
Hall (top row, second
from left) and fellow
officers of 5/South
Wales Borderers,
c. 1915.
(RWF Museum)

44   TNA WO339/58123: Lt. CE Lyon-Hall service record.

7

57 Brigade

Whilst 58 Brigade was attacking La Boisselle's underbelly from the south-east on 2 July, into the 3rd, 57 Brigade launched its assault during the early hours of the 3rd from the north-east, in conjunction with the 12th Division's frontal attack on Ovillers across Mash Valley. At a conference of commanding officers of 57 Brigade at battalion HQ on 2 July, 8/North Staffords and 10/Worcesters received orders to make an advance on La Boisselle if 58 Brigade failed to clear the village. (In this operation, 8/Glosters would be in support whilst 10/Royal Warwicks held the British front line, ready to be called forward if needed). At 2:50 am on the 3rd, some confusion reigned as an individual had apparently shouted 'About turn and double!'.[1] The 57th Infantry Brigade's war diary reveals that 'Col. de Wyat' [Colonel Adrian Carton de Wiart, CO of 8/Glosters] steadied the men of 8/North Staffords and kept them going forward as per instructions.

The war diary of the latter battalion made a note that the deployment of troops at this moment was 'too hurried', and 'no time was allowed to explain to the men what was required of them'. It went on:

> The first party to go over was one platoon of D Coy under 2/Lt. Hunter. They went over about 4.5 a.m. and seized the crater in front of the La Boisselle salient [Y Sap crater, Figure 9.1] before the bombers entered. The Bn. swept up the village and trenches fairly easily at first, up to a point about 3/4 way up. Having reached this far, the bomb supply began to [run] out, although Bn. HQ men formed a carrying party. By this time about 100 of the enemy had surrendered.[2]

The narrative goes on to say that, in tandem with other battalions of the brigade, following the depletion of the grenade supply, a German counter-attack pushed them back to a position only a short way inside the village itself. Enemy snipers had already

---

1   TNA WO95/2083: 57 Brigade War Diary.
2   TNA WO95/2085: 8/North Staffs. Regt. War Diary.

Figure 9.1 Y Sap Crater, on the edge of La Boisselle, photographed on 3 July 1916. Shells are bursting in the distance over German lines. The British forward trench is in the foreground. Y Sap had caused many problems to the British since their arrival in July 1915, and its destruction was widely acclaimed. (Copyright: Imperial War Museum Q69)

been targeting officers and other leaders, but a concerted push, aided by reinforcements, drove the Germans backwards once more. By 8 am, a more efficient system of carrying supplies into La Boisselle had been established, although isolated groups were still engaged in their own fierce fights, often unaided. Dug-outs were systematically cleared by ruthless means, and one of the communication trenches leading to Ovillers – which was still under siege by the 12th Division – was secured. It was later 'blocked', but German reinforcements sent up to assist in the defence succeeded in breaking down the temporary barrier and launching their own offensive manoeuvre, driving the British back to a line running approximately half way through the hamlet. This position, close to the church, was maintained from around 12 noon on the 3rd until dawn on the following day. Another criticism made in the North Staffordshires' war diary was the equipment failure when transporting Lewis gun magazines into action. Poor stitching and riveting in the men's packs had caused the drums to fall out at critical moments, so a series of dumps had to be set up whereby the machine-gun crews could replenish their stocks. Exhausted, 58 Brigade was withdrawn on 4 July

Major Cecil Wedgwood, DSO
8th Battalion, North Staffordshire
Regiment
Killed in action 3 July 1916

The commanding officer of the battalion
at La Boisselle, responsible for the welfare
of all ranks, Major Wedgwood, DSO
[Figure 9.2] was a well known figure in his
home county, both as a business man and
soldier. Born at Trentham, Staffordshire,
during 1863, he was descended from
Josiah Wedgwood, the famous potter
and chinaware manufacturer. Cecil
Wedgwood attended Clifton College
in Bristol before finishing his education at Geneva University. It was during
this varied education that he encountered Douglas Haig, a fellow school-
mate. Wedgewood joined the family firm
in 1882, was married to Lucie six years
later, and became part of the local militia,
leading to his period of active service

Figure 9.2 Major C. Wedgewood DSO.
(*Birmingham Weekly Post*)

during the Boer War (1899–1902). He was military commandant in several locales,
mentioned in despatches twice, and bestowed with the Distinguished Service Order
for services rendered during the South African War.

Returning to his civilian role, he was highly regarded by all levels of society, especially those who worked under him, and he was appointed the first mayor of the
Stoke-on-Trent county borough in 1910. It was said that he recognised the rising
threat of Germany from an early stage, and as soon as war broke out, he applied
himself rigorously to the recruitment of local men [Figure 9.3]. He was eventually
promoted to major in his home regiment, and although his age was against him, he
was permitted to sail overseas with many of the soldiers he had first encouraged to join
up. (7/North Staffordshire Regiment was up to strength within just eight days during
September 1914, whilst the 8th reached its capacity after ten).

Originally second-in-command of the 8th Battalion, Major Wedgwood was its CO
on 3 July 1916, owing to an illness which befell the colonel. Numerous eye-witness
accounts of the major's final moments survive. The *History of 8th North Staffords* recounts
how enemy agents had issued a fake order to the British to 'retire' as the attack on La
Boisselle had reached 3/4 of the way into the village. Realising his men were faltering,
Major Wedgwood leapt onto the parapet of a German trench, regardless of personal
danger, shouting: 'Forward, North Staffords!' He was then struck by a sniper's bullet
and died almost immediately. The enemy counter-attack, mentioned in the war diary,

then drove the British line back before it consolidated near the church. The loss of their commanding officer must have been a huge blow to his men, who had implicit confidence in him. These soldiers, as well as his grieving family, could all relate to the following epitaph: '[He] sacrificed his life in a cause in which he sincerely and profoundly believed, and for him at least there would have been no regrets at the manner of his death'.[3]

Other reports more or less agree the major was shot in the neck, although the time it happened varies between early morning and the afternoon. (The war diary states it was at 6 am, just as the counter attack began).

A memorial service and special borough meetings were held in Stoke to mark the passing of one of the area's most distinguished sons. At the former, where hundreds of current and past employees were in attendance alongside family members and civic dignitaries, it was said of him: 'Major Wedgwood's was a fine record of public life, because the domi-

Figure 9.3 Major Wedgwood at a recruiting meeting, c. autumn 1914. (Staffordshire Weekly Sentinel)

nant thought about him in men's minds was that he could be trusted, and they knew with absolute certainty that he never sought his own interests, but stood for the good of the community'.[4]

The Stoke-on-Trent borough council wished to place on record their sincere condolences to Major Wedgwood's widow and children, and also paid tribute to his sterling efforts in all matters of local public life. With regard to his army career, it was noted that the major had the opportunity to take up a staff appointment prior to the Somme offensive, but he declined, preferring to stay with 'his own battalion and his own folk'. When war was declared, Major Wedgwood had ventured: '"Well, I hope they will send me somewhere where I shall be useful". He had gone, and they [the citizens of Stoke-on-Trent] all felt the loss, but if the example he had set had left its impression on their loss, then, indeed, Major Wedgwood had achieved something'.[5] His body

3   *Staffordshire Advertiser* newspaper, 8 July 1916.
4   Ibid.
5   Ibid.

now lies at the Bapaume Post Military Cemetery, on the main road leaving Albert before reaching La Boisselle. At fifty-three, he was one of the 19th Division's most senior casualties in age during the attack.

Major James Carnegy
8th Battalion, North Staffordshire
Regiment
Killed in action 3 July 1916

Figure 9.4 Major J. Carnegy.
(Staffordshire Regiment Museum)

Just after 4 am on 3 July, the leading platoon of 8/North Staffords reached the Y Sap Crater, and, believing it was still held by the enemy, threw grenades into its depths. Some of the soldiers following behind became disorientated, thinking that the explosions were German in origin, and started to hesitate. Major Carnegy [Figure 9.4] then went in front of his men, waved his stick in the air and shouted 'Come on Staffords!, enabling the advance to continue into the village. An hour later, he reported that his battalion, along with 10/Worcesters, had made contact with units of 58 Brigade in La Boisselle. At 6 am, the major – who was in command of B Company – was killed by a German sniper.

Born in the East Indies on 21 July 1875, James Carnegy was the son of Patrick Carnegy, a soon to be major general of the Madras Army, and his wife, Kate. Educated at the United Services College in Westward Ho!, Devon (an institution set up for the sons of army officers to prepare its students for military life), he joined a militia battalion of the Royal Dublin Fusiliers in 1898 before transferring to 1/North Staffordshires two years later, serving during the Boer War. His father died in the Stroud area of Gloucestershire during 1902, and his widow later moved to Newnham-on-Severn in the same county. On the former's headstone at Edge parish church, near Stroud, Major Carnegy is also mentioned: 'He lies interred at La Boisselle, France, where he gallantly fell in action on 3rd July 1916 in his 41st year. There is but one task for all/ For each one life to give/ Who stands if Freedom fall/ Who dies if England live'.

The major is remembered at Thiepval.

Second Lieutenant William Lawton
8th Battalion, North Staffordshire
Killed in action 3 July 1916

Born at Hanley, near Stoke-on-Trent, in
1896, William [Figure 9.5] was the son of
William senior – a designer and modeller
for pottery – and Mary. He was educated
at Hanley secondary school, followed by
the Victoria University in Manchester,
where he became a member of the Officer
Training Corps. He received his commission in February 1915, and proceeded to
France the following April.

The *History of the 8th North Staffords*
does not give any indication as to how
Second Lieutenant Lawton lost his life on
3 July 1916, but does mention:

Figure 9.5 Second Lieutenant W. Lawton.
(*Staffordshire Weekly Sentinel*)

> Many unrecorded acts of bravery and devotion to duty were performed. The
> entire action, in fact, resolved itself into a series of individual efforts of Junior
> Officers and Men, rather than a concentrated action. The Battalion had been
> split into small parties from the start of the attack, and remained so until it was
> relieved. In spite of this enormous handicap it had succeeded in penetrating the
> enemy's stronghold.[6]

Aged twenty, Second Lieutenant Lawton is another to be commemorated at
Thiepval.

6   Crewe, F, *The History of the 8th North Staffords* (Stoke-on-Trent: Hughes & Harber 1921),
     p. 48.

Figure 9.6 Mash Valley today, looking towards Ovillers (the spire of the modern church can
be seen on the left-hand horizon). The houses mark the German front line on 2/3 July 1916.
Whilst the 12th Division attacked Ovillers (this photograph was taken close to the British
front line of the same date), 57 Brigade of 19th Division passed Y Sap crater (now filled in,
but situated centre foreground) and entered La Boisselle beyond the line of trees on the right.
Compare this image with that of Y Sap crater in Figure 9.1. (Author's collection)

Second Lieutenant William George Fletcher
11th (attached 8th) Battalion, North Staffordshire Regiment
Killed in action 3 July 1916

In the official casualty rolls, Second Lieutenant Fletcher is listed as serving with 2/
South Lancashire Regiment, which was fighting nearby at the time, but his name
appears within the officer deaths of 8/North Staffords. Born in Middlesex on 28
February 1894, William was the son of Robert and Nora, who both hailed from
Birmingham. Educated at Highgate School and in France, he was a medical student
at the London Hospital [Figure 9.7] when war was declared. In his service record[7]
there is a reference to him spending three months on the Western Front with the BEF,
attached to an Australian Voluntary Hospital from 20 August until 23 November

7   TNA WO339/33400: 2/Lt. WG Fletcher service record.

1914, the period which covered the opening phases of the conflict.

Sailing back to the UK, he received his commission with the North Staffordshire Regiment on 28 January 1915, and later returned to the front with the South Lancashires. The London Hospital archives note that he was 'killed in action while bombing during the attack on La Boisselle 3rd–6th July 1916', whilst the *History of 8th North Staffords* describes him as the battalion's 'Bombing Officer'. In the confusion of battle, Captain Standbridge, the adjutant when the battalion proceeded to France, wrote to Second Lieutenant Fletcher's mother informing her that her son had been wounded and was now in hospital in London. He later contacted her and apologised for his error. (Eight officers were injured in addition to the four fatalities. Captain Standbridge had clearly misheard the fate of the twenty-two year old subaltern).

Figure 9.7 Second Lieutenant W. G. Fletcher. (London Hospital)

As with his three officer comrades, it seems likely Second Lieutenant Fletcher managed to reach as far as the ruins of La Boisselle before he was killed in the close-quarter fight. His body was not recovered to be identified, so he is remembered at Thiepval.

The *History of 8th North Staffords* revealed:

> The trench system in the village was so complicated that it was difficult even in daytime to identify points marked on the map, especially as many of the trenches had been wholly or partially destroyed by the successive bombardments and numerous mines which had sprung up round the apex of the salient [the Glory Hole]. Practically nothing remained of the houses in the village. The ground was so torn by shell fire that in the dark the remains of the trenches and the shell craters were almost indistinguishable. The defences had been heavily wired, and the remains of this wire lay everywhere.

The battalion war diary also makes a reference to the weight of the packs and equipment each soldier had to carry – sixty-nine pounds (nearly five stone, or thirty-one kilograms). This included bombs, small arms ammunition, a pick or a shovel, their rifle, entrenching tool, food, rations and water, etc. In addition, some carried wire-cutters, others flares, and most had to transport two sandbags across No Man's Land. With four platoons to each company, two Lewis gun teams accompanied them, along with two bombing squads of five men each. Four men from each platoon were detailed to form a carrying party, leaving approximately twenty men to complete a platoon of fighting soldiers. From this, six individuals became company runners (messengers between the forward lines and battalion HQ), and each officer had his own personal orderly. Thus the breakdown was as follows: 'Four Companies – 640; Lewis gunners – 56; bombers – 34; runners – 36; signallers – 16; police – 8. Total strength on 1st July 1916 – 790'. Twelve officers and 272 other ranks had become casualties by 4 July.[8]

As 10/Worcesters were being brought up for the attack on 2 July, carrying parties were struggling along the rain-soaked communication trenches in both directions, and all were obliged to move aside for the many hundreds of wounded of the 34th Division who were being evacuated from the battlefield after the previous day's fighting. Advancing past Y Sap crater and into La Boisselle alongside 8/North Staffords in the darkness of early morning on 3 July, the *Worcestershire Regiment in the Great War* describes the scene:

> In and around the smashed heaps of masonry which had once been houses, the British platoons fought with enemies who appeared suddenly and unexpectedly from every side. Only by the momentary light of flares and shell-bursts was it possible to distinguish friend from foe. The fighting was hand-to-hand or at point blank range, with bomb, bullet or cold steel.[9]

It went on to declare: 'The 10th Worcestershires had every reason to be proud of their first battle; for the captured position was of immense strength. The dugouts were so deep and of such solid construction that even after the terrific bombardment of the previous week many of them were still undamaged; and the defenders.... had fought to the last'. Of the 153 prisoners taken by 57 Brigade, nearly all were wounded. As the fight for La Boisselle continued, individual German posts were gradually isolated, surrounded and eventually eliminated by concerted British attacks, but the cost to 10/Worcesters – raised in its county town during September 1914 – was once again high.

8   TNA WO95/2085: 8/North Staffs. Regt. War Diary.
9   Stacke, Capt. HF, *The Worcestershire Regiment in the Great War* (Uckfield: The Naval & Military Press Ltd, reprint, 2002), p. 170.

Lieutenant Colonel George Arthur Royston-Pigott, DSO
Commanding Officer of 10th Battalion, Worcestershire Regiment (attached from Northamptonshire Regiment)
Killed in action 3 July 1916

Once the infantry had gone over, the CO, Lieutenant Colonel Royston-Pigott, made his way forward to the Y Sap crater, alongside his adjutant – Captain Gillum-Webb – to establish the battalion's whereabouts in La Boisselle. He dictated a message to his captain, reporting the progress back to brigade HQ, and just as he finished its content, he was shot through the heart. (The adjutant was wounded shortly afterwards, leaving the remaining officers in the fighting line to press home the assault).

Figure 9.8 Lieutenant Colonel G. Royston-Pigott (Author's collection)

Born in Surrey on 18 December 1874, George Royston-Pigott [Figure 9.8] was the eldest son of Dr GW Royston-Pigott, FRS, and Agnes. He was an officer cadet at Sandhurst and became a second lieutenant with the Northamptonshire Regiment in 1895. He saw much action during the Boer War (1899–1902) and was appointed adjutant of his battalion during 1912. He was second-in-command of 1/Northants in May 1915, and took part in operations at Loos the following September, for which he was awarded a Distinguished Service Order as well as being mentioned in despatches. Now a temporary lieutenant colonel, he was given the command of 10/Worcesters in February 1916.

He married Hilda Parriss in 1915, and she placed notices in *The Times* on the date of his death for a number of years, once quoting James Russell Lowell's poem *Memoriae Positum* ('memory'). Her husband, who was aged forty-one, lies buried at the Ovillers Military Cemetery, within sight of Y Sap crater where he lost his life.

Major Frederick St George Tucker
10th Battalion, Worcestershire Regiment
Killed in action 3 July 1916

Figure 9.9 Major Frederick St George Tucker. (Jane Jones WWI Photos)

> He is loved, admired and respected by all ranks. He never sends an officer, N.C.O. or man to a post without first going himself and sampling it as to danger... When the firing is the hottest, Major Tucker is found giving cheery words to his men and confidence by his presence.[10]

So wrote one of the major's sergeants in the forward line before the officer's death at the age of thirty-three. Born in India on 27 February 1883, Frederick [Figure 9.9] was the son of Frederick senior, of the Royal Artillery. Educated at Haileybury, he joined the Worcestershire Regiment as a second lieutenant in 1902 and steadily rose through the ranks, spending a year prior to the war serving with the Royal Flying Corps, which had only been established in 1912. During his time in Sierra Leone, he was awarded the Royal Humane Society's Medal for saving a native from drowning in a crocodile-infested river.

In June 1915, just days after being promoted to major, he married Eileen Baker, and twelve months later he was mentioned in General Sir Douglas Haig's despatch for gallantry in the field. On 3 July 1916, it is possible Major Tucker led 10/Worcesters into the attack on La Boisselle which took his life. His body now lies buried next to his Commanding Officer, Lieutenant Colonel Royston-Pigott, DSO, and other comrades at Ovillers Military Cemetery.

---

10   De Ruvigny, Marquis, *Roll of Honour 1914–18 Vol. II* (Uckfield: The Naval & Military Press Ltd, reprint, 2001), p. 299.

Captain Richard Greaves Tasker
10th Battalion, Worcestershire Regiment
Killed in action 3 July 1916

In 1958, a Sergeant F Thomas, of an unspecified regiment, gained possession of a wrist watch which bore the inscription on the reverse: 'Lt. R.G. Tasker, Worcestershire Regiment'.[11] It had been in the possession of a German prisoner of war (presumably World War Two), and it is only a supposition that the father of the POW either fought at La Boisselle in 1916, or knew of someone who did. The timepiece may have been taken from the officer's body after the counter-attack on the morning of 3 July, as this was the only time that ground secured by the 19th Division was regained by the Germans before they, too, were systematically

Figure 9.10 Captain R.G. Tasker.
(Author's collection)

driven out of the village. It is therefore also an assumption that Captain Tasker fell shortly before or just after 57 Brigade had reached its furthest point early on in the assault.

Born at Stow-on-the-Wold, Gloucestershire, [the Commonwealth War Graves Commission indicates he was a native of Worcester, but this information is not supported by other records][12] on 7 July 1888, he was the son of Greaves and Julia. He attended Bromsgrove School and then Worcester College, Oxford, where he gained honours in Classical Moderations and Law with a view to becoming a solicitor. Setting aside his studies as a student of the Inner Temple, in the heart of the City of London, he received his commission with the Worcestershire Regiment (having already served in the OTC at Oxford), and he married Vera Merrett at the beginning of 1915. Their son, Anthony, was born in March 1916, by which time Richard [Figure 9.10] had already been promoted to captain.

After the fighting at La Boisselle, his body was identified by the disc which each serviceman carried on his person for such a grim eventuality, and his grave can also be found at the Ovillers Military Cemetery. The watch was presumably a token of affection from his wife or other family members, and he died just four days before his twenty-eighth birthday.

11   TNA WO339/56246: Capt. RG Tasker service record.
12   Online birth details: www.freebmd.org.uk & officer's service record – see 11.

Captain Alexander Reginald Thomas, DCM
10th Battalion, Worcestershire Regiment
Killed in action 3 July 1916

> SOUTHAMPTON D.S.O.* HERO KILLED.
> FINE RECORD OF CAPTAIN ALEC THOMAS. [*This should be DCM]
>
> News has been received by his mother at Southampton of the death in action of
> Captain Alec R. Thomas, second son of Mrs. [Mariam] Thomas, of St. Bedes…
> He was attached to the Worcestershire Regiment, and met his death whilst
> leading his men into action for bomb throwing on the 3rd of this month. Captain
> Thomas won three [campaign] medals whilst serving in [South Africa], and was
> in India when the present [war] commenced, but immediately returned home
> and joined his regiment [15th Hussars]. He has been mentioned three times in
> despatches, and later won the [DCM] for conspicuous gallantry in the field. On
> one occasion he saved his battalion from being cut up, and on another he carried
> a major and several men to safety under heavy fire from the enemy.[13]

Born in Dorchester, Dorset, in 1882 (his birth was registered as 'Aleck Reginald'),
he later moved to Dover with his family before settling in Southampton. His father,
Walter, was a civil engineer and architect. Alec served in the Hampshire Yeomanry for
twelve years prior to the Great War, and later joined the 15th Hussars, going to France
with them in November 1914. 'He took part in many battles, including Ypres, and
was awarded the DCM for gallantry in May 1915'.[14] He received his commission the
following September, and undertook training in France to become a bombing officer.

On leave several weeks before the Somme offensive began, Captain Thomas
returned to the Western Front to take part in the attack on La Boisselle: 'He was last
seen alive on the field, urging his men forward, and shouting words of encouragement
in the face of a terrific hail of lead from the enemy'.[15] In April 1917, the War Office
informed his family that his body had been '…buried just outside the south-western
end of La Boisselle village. The grave has been marked by a durable wooden cross with
an inscription bearing full particulars'.[16] (This location was approximately, therefore,
in the vicinity of the pre-war civilian burial ground, close to the Glory Hole). Today,
his final resting place is several miles away at the Pozières British Cemetery, between
La Boisselle and Bapaume.

One of his sisters enquired of the War Office as to the whereabouts of his
Distinguished Conduct Medal, but the official reply is not to hand.

---

13   *Hampshire Independent* newspaper, 15 July 1916.
14   TNA WO339/43078: Capt. AR Thomas service record.
15   *Hampshire Independent* newspaper, 15 July 1916.
16   TNA WO339/43078: Capt. AR Thomas service record.

Figure 9.11 The Pozières British Cemetery, which lies on the main road to Bapaume. The village of Pozières was a target of 1 July 1916, but did not fall into British hands until the 24th of the same month.

Lieutenant Richard William Jennings
10th Battalion, Worcestershire Regiment
Died of wounds 3 July 1916

The final hours of Lieutenant Jennings [Figure 9.12] are well-documented, as the man who stayed with him as he lay mortally wounded, and then carried him back to the British lines, was awarded his country's highest honour for valour.

Richard Jennings was born at King's Stanley rectory, near Stroud, Gloucestershire, on 6 March 1889. His parents were Reverend Arthur Jennings, the parish priest, and Isabella. Their son was educated at Bradfield College, Berkshire, and Jesus College, Cambridge, where he studied law, becoming a qualified solicitor in due course. (At university he was the lightweight boxing champion 1909–10, and was a fine all-round athlete,

Figure 9.12 Lieutenant R.W. Jennings. (Author's collection)

taking part in Alpine pursuits including the Creston toboggan run).

Joining the ranks of 10/Worcesters in September 1914, he was soon commissioned into the same battalion, proceeding with them to France the following year. Mentioned in General Haig's despatches for gallant and distinguished services in the field during mid-June 1916, he took part in the attack on La Boisselle on 3 July. Once amid the ruins of the village, Lieutenant Jennings led one of the bombing parties, which had been specially trained for such engagements. Originally labelled a 'grenadier platoon', they were later known simply as 'bombers', due to the Grenadier Guards – one of the elite and most historic of British regiments – objecting to the widespread use of their official title in all units. Accompanying Lieutenant Jennings was, amongst others, Private Thomas Turrall, and when the former was struck down with several injuries, Private Turrall dragged the officer into a shell-hole before bandaging his wounds. As he did so, a group of Germans started throwing grenades at the stranded duo, whereupon Private Turrall fired at the assailants, forcing them back [Figure 9.13].

Figure 9.13 Artist's impression of Private Turrall's deed. (Naval & Military Press)

However, from his vantage point, the private could see a wave of German infantry pouring forward from the direction of Pozières – the strong counter-attack mentioned previously which forced the British back during the morning of 3 July. Feigning death, Private Turrall was prodded with bayonets as the enemy pressed onwards, leaving both men (Lieutenant Jennings was drifting in and out of consciousness by this time) now isolated behind the fighting line. Throughout the day, Private Turrall faithfully kept at Lieutenant Jennings' side, under heavy fire, and then, remarkably, after dark, he was able to carry the officer on his back towards their own lines, aided by the secondary surge made by the 19th Division in the afternoon which secured more ground within La Boisselle. (Fearing German subterfuge, the pair were *both* challenged to raise their hands by British sentries when they returned, not realising that Lieutenant Jennings was in a state of collapse. Fortunately, they were allowed through).

Figure 9.14 Private T. Turrall VC.
(Author's collection)

Twenty-seven year old Lieutenant Jennings was taken to 103 Field Ambulance, where he revived for just long enough to dictate the account of his rescuer's bravery before he succumbed to his injuries. As a direct result of this letter, Private Turrall [Figure 9.14] was awarded the Victoria Cross. The soldier's own version of events was transcribed in a communication[17] he sent to the deceased officer's parents, in which he commented that Lieutenant Jennings '… led our company with unflinching pluck', and adding that the first dugout they came to was dealt with by a grenade thrown by the officer himself. As the small group progressed deeper into the village, they discovered that the Germans had withdrawn to enable them to provide stronger resistance further back, and soon opened fire. Despite being shot in his left arm, Lieutenant Jennings continued before receiving a bomb wound to his right thigh, leading to a brother officer recommending he sought medical aid. He refused, and after Private Turrall had pulled him into the shell-hole, several more bombs shattered the officer's left leg, and further damaged his right knee.

17   *Gloucester Journal* newspaper, 16 September 1916.

The private then constructed an improvised splint using his entrenching tool handle and his puttees for bandages.

The chaplain of 103 Field Ambulance informed Reverend and Mrs Jennings that their son had died 'quietly and peacefully' on the operating table, before the medical staff could try and save him. In response to Private Turrall's letter, Isabella Jennings wrote to the soldier's parents in Birmingham and told them: '… when [your son] is home in England I will go anywhere…to see him, and give him some special thing in memory of Lieut. Jennings…'[18] (Private Turrall received his VC from the King at Buckingham Palace on 30 December 1916, but by this time the devastated Jennings family had left King's Stanley parish after thirty years' dedicated service. Before moving, they commissioned a brass plaque within the church, stating their officer son was '…fatally wounded leading the Company to the capture of La Boisselle in the Battle of the Somme July 3rd 1916'.

Lieutenant Jennings is buried at the Meaulte Military Cemetery, due south of Albert. Had Private Turrall, VC, not shown such extraordinary devotion to duty, the officer's body may have been lost entirely. The VC recipient, who survived the conflict, was congratulated by the Lord Mayor of Birmingham – Alderman Neville Chamberlain (the future Prime Minister at the outbreak of the Second World War) – who expressed his pride at the thirty year old's gallant exploits.

Whilst this book primarily focuses upon the officers of the 19th Division, the contributions and sacrifices of the men who followed them into battle should not, of course, be overlooked. Lance Corporal AJ Gardner, 10/Worcesters, for example, was awarded a Distinguished Conduct Medal for conspicuous gallantry in action at La Boisselle on 3 July: 'He went forward alone with a machine gun in front of the advancing infantry, firing as he ran with the gun under his arm at a party of the enemy. He was wounded, but went on firing till he fainted from loss of blood'.[19]

Private Victor Weaver, 8/Glosters (whose battalion was sent forward in support of the North Staffordshires and Worcesters at a critical moment on 3 July, described later in this chapter) was soon reported 'wounded and missing', and his subaltern subsequently wrote to the soldier's parents:

> Your son was amongst the first to jump over the parapet and go forward towards the enemy position. He was with me through all the attacks … and repeatedly showed extreme bravery in carrying messages to his CO [Lieutenant Colonel Carton de Wiart], going across open country and being all the time in full view of the enemy and under a hot fire. Whilst you have lost a dutiful son, I have lost a comrade whom I was awfully proud of, and no words can express adequately how I feel his absence. He was really invaluable. There is one consolation … [that] he

---

18   Ibid.
19   *London Gazette* citation, 22 September 1916, L/Cpl Gardner DCM.

Figure 9.15 Soldiers of 10/Worcesters escort German prisoners to the rear on 3 July 1916. The POWs had endured the week long artillery bombardment followed by a three day infantry battle, whilst the British had just suffered heavy losses in the capture of La Boisselle. The men in the foreground portray the suffering of both sides. (© Imperial War Museum Q763)

died the finest death a man can die, for King and Country. He was a man who knew no fears.[20]

Lieutenant Campbell Keith, also of 8/Glosters, told the family of Lance Corporal Arthur Berryman, who fell on 3 July, that '…he was of inestimable value during the fight at La Boisselle, and the way in which he bombed the Germans out of their trenches and dug-outs was particularly fine and brave'.[21] The same officer said of Private Melsome, another casualty: 'He was assisting our Medical Officer in the work of picking up the wounded from between the lines when he was hit in the head by a bullet which was either a stray [shot], or one fired by a German sniper… He was invaluable as a stretcher bearer and no one could have done his work better than he did, for, regardless of his own safety he attended to the wounded unceasingly until he fell'.[22] Men in the ranks also often described the captured enemy trenches, initially

20   *Gloucester Journal* newspaper, 22 July 1916.
21   Ibid. 15 July 1916.
22   Ibid.

astounded at the differences between their own: 'The Germans, when they built dug-outs like subterranean villas, comfortably furnished and with electric light, thought they were there to stay, but the sands of miscalculation are slowly running out'.[23]

Another likened the underground shelters to a 'dressing room in a hotel', noting the presence of electricity, a water pump, an abundance of clean linen, spare boots, washing and shaving gear, cigars, cigarettes and food.[24] (The essentials of nourishment and drinking water, of course, became scarcer from 24 June 1916 until the final capture of La Boisselle).

Surviving British officers were sometimes the first to break bad news to their soldiers' next of kin. Private Fred Nelmes, 10/Worcesters, did not answer the battalion roll call after the attack on the village, and Captain Bernard Ellis informed his anxious family back in the Forest of Dean:

> I do not think there is any hope he is a prisoner…as the Germans were driven back and the battlefield is in our hands. Three out of four of his Company who went into action were killed, and four of his platoon. None of his comrades here saw him wounded, and all I can gather is that he was last seen on the German side of No Man's Land. It might be some comfort to know that he was respected and liked by his officers and comrades.[25]

Lieutenant Cecil Henry Gossett Lushington
10th Battalion, Worcestershire Regiment
Killed in action 3 July 1916

Born in India on 16 December 1884, he was the younger son of Major and Mrs AJ Lushington, who later returned to England with the rest of their family. Cecil was educated at Haileybury College, Hertfordshire [Figure 9.16], and he became a fine cricketer, hockey and lawn tennis player. When war broke out, he was employed in growing fruit at Pershore in Worcestershire, and he immediately applied for a commission in his local county regiment. During

Figure 9.16 Lieutenant C.H.G. Lushington. (Haileybury College)

23   Ibid. 13 July 1916.
24   Ibid.
25   *Dean Forest Mercury* newspaper, 28 July 1916.

February 1915, he married Evelyn Hirst of Bampton, Oxfordshire, and went with his battalion to France the following July, receiving a promotion to lieutenant in October.

In the absence of official notification (other than their son was 'missing'), Lieutenant Lushington's family endeavoured to piece together their own version of events,[26] which led them to provide what they deemed to be 'conclusive proof that he is no longer alive':

> From officers and men in the Regt., we have learnt that the 10th Worcesters attacked La Boiselle at dawn on the 3rd July last, my son being one of the party, and apparently before reaching the first line of German trenches, heavy casualties occurred, the Comdg. Officer [Royston-Pigott], the Major Comdg. my son's Company [Tucker], & others, being killed, & my son was 'knocked over' but declined help, and proceeded with his Company, & was seen fighting in the village of La Boisselle between 4 & 5 a.m. The village seems to have been surrounded by a network of barbed wire & trenches – some of which had not been cleared, and according to the report of a wounded Sergeant of the Regt., Lieut. Lushington led a party of men in pursuit of the Germans, bombing them, for some distance, but on reaching a traverse, the Germans threw bombs which wounded Lieut. Lushington in both legs…

Here, the tangible evidence subsides. Two of the officer's group who were also injured were subsequently evacuated, and their testimonies state that Lieutenant Lushington sent his own 'runner' – Private Burgess – on with the rest of the platoon, telling him he would fend for himself. When Private Burgess returned to the same spot, the lieutenant was not there, and it was suggested that he had last been seen crawling back towards his own lines, but no further definite sightings of him could be gleaned.

Major Lushington placed a great deal of credence in the eye-witness report of Rifleman Watson, of 2/Royal Irish Rifles, which was attached to the 12th Division in readiness for an attack on neighbouring Ovillers. As Rifleman Watson was assisting a wounded officer of the Cheshires to a dressing station, he saw another stricken officer and went to his aid, bringing him under cover into a communication trench. The latter, who was dying, gave Watson several personal items from his tunic, including a silver cigarette case, a card inscribed with Lieutenant Lushington's name and the address of his wife in Bampton, plus a number of photographs. The officer died as Rifleman Watson was tending to him, and the effects were later passed on to a Red Cross nurse in Etaples, France, who forwarded them on to Major Lushington back in England. Although he himself was wounded, Watson believed the date of this incident was on or about 5 July. The rifleman also stated the time of Lieutenant Lushington's death was 10:20 am, and that the wound which finally accounted for

---

26   TNA WO339/14528: Lt. CHG Lushington service record.

the officer was caused by shrapnel which burst close by and penetrated the base of his skull. '*This occurred near Fricourt, about 1.5 to 1.75 miles from La Boiselle, where he was first wounded in the legs*' [author's italics], wrote Major Lushington in his letter to the authorities. This is puzzling, although it may be Watson's generalisation of the *area* in which they were fighting, rather than mistaking the location as being somewhere other than La Boisselle. It is a dubious assumption that after being wounded, Lieutenant Lushington somehow made his way to Fricourt where he was injured for the final time.

Another discrepancy lies with the date on which both men were in action, as Lieutenant Lushington undoubtedly went forward with 10/Worcesters across Mash Valley and into La Boisselle on 3 July, whereas 2/Royal Irish Rifles attacked Ovillers on the 7th. It is unlikely that any officers would still be left injured and unattended in La Boisselle by 7 July, as all of it by then was in British hands. However, Rifleman Watson, who may have been attached to another unit altogether, clearly encountered the lieutenant at some stage, as he was given the officer's belongings by which he could be identified. The War Office later confirmed that in view of the evidence and circumstantial reports, the death was accepted for official purposes as having occurred 'on or about 3rd July 1916'. (The thirty-one year old does not have a known grave, and he is remembered at Thiepval. Is it possible that in his delirium he crawled towards German-held Ovillers, instead of the British lines, and was not found for several days? Yet an unofficial source in an Evesham newspaper claimed he had died almost straight away after being injured. A mystery indeed).

One of Major Lushington's reasons for establishing the day on which his son died lay in his desire to place a commemorative plaque in Bampton Church. It was said of the lieutenant:

> The service has lost one of its best officers; he was so conscientious in everything he undertook, and so keen on his work; a most dependable officer, and liked and respected by all who knew him'. Another wrote: 'He was a splendid officer, and his men always loved him and would have followed him anywhere. He had the very highest form of courage; he realised danger, but never shirked it.[27]

27 *Evesham Journal* newspaper, 5 August 1916.

Second Lieutenant George Major Solloway Foster
10th Battalion, Worcestershire Regiment
Killed in action 3 July 1916

Originally reported 'wounded' on 3 July, he was later confirmed to have been killed on that date. Born at Dudley, Worcestershire, on 14 March 1888, George [Figure 9.17] was the son of George and Eleanor, and attended the local grammar school before training to become an accountant in Birmingham. Joining 16/Royal Warwickshire Regiment (3rd Birmingham Pals) at the outbreak of war, he was later commissioned from the ranks into the Worcesters.

In 1920, his parents were informed that his body had been exhumed from an 'isolated grave' to the west of Ovillers-la-Boisselle (this was probably close to the site originally called Mash Valley Cemetery) and re-interred at 'Ovillers British Cemetery' (now known as the Military Cemetery). This was the policy of the (then) Imperial War Graves Commission, which amalgamated small and scattered burial grounds into larger, more manageable places of interment after the conflict had ended.

Figure 9.17 Lieutenant G.M.S. Foster.
(*Dudley Herald*)

A watch and a cheque book belonging to the fallen twenty-eight year old officer were returned to his family.

Second Lieutenant Cyril Vernon Hadley
10th Battalion, Worcestershire Regiment
Killed in action 3 July 1916

FORMER WESTON SCHOOLMASTER POSTED AS WOUNDED AND MISSING.

Considerable anxiety is occasioned among a wide circle of local friends and acquaintances with the fact that Lieut. C.V. Hadley... late assistant master of Kingsholme School, in this town [Weston-super-mare], is posted as wounded and missing. Lieut. Hadley is a huge favourite, not only in local cricket and football arenas, but in every social and professional relationship…[28]

Second Lieutenant Hadley's name was passed on to the American Embassy, which assisted in the tracing of 'missing' British officers and men by circulating details through as many German hospitals and internment camps as was feasible. His fate, however, seemed fairly defined from an early stage, as Private Overthrow declared from his hospital bed: '… [at] about 1:30 – 2 a.m. at Fricourt [another reference to the nearby village, when the actual location was La Boisselle] in an attack, when about 50 yards from [our] objective [which was] a German trench, I saw Lieut. C. Hadley fall, knocked over in very marshy ground[29] and long grass'.[30]

Private Overthrow was then wounded by shrapnel close to the German lines and saw no more of Second Lieutenant Hadley, whilst Private Meakin revealed: 'At Albert we made an advance at the break of day. Lieut. Hadley was leading his platoon, He was struck by a bomb and fell at the German barbed wire, dead. I believe he was a school master by profession'.[31] Private Workman concurred: 'Lt. Hadley reached the German barbed wire and was bombed and seen to fall'.[32] Private Collins agreed with the other statements, adding that the Salvage Corps soon went out and buried all the bodies they could find in and around La Boisselle, although their task was not to stop or take identification discs from the corpses, as they had to work hastily due to active enemy snipers. In addition, detailed reports were not compiled due to the dangerous nature of their occupation.

Cyril was born in Birmingham during 1896, the son of Frederick and Ellen. He was educated at King Edward's School in the city between 1907 and 1912, and soon began his training to become a teacher. Enlisting as a sapper in the 2nd Wessex Company of the Royal Engineers during September 1914, his commission into the Worcesters came about twelve months later, after he had spent the first winter of the war in the trenches.

In May 1917, it was accepted for official purposes that twenty year old Second Lieutenant Hadley had been killed 'on or since' 3 July 1916. It may seem strange to our modern perspective that in such a confined space as La Boisselle, individuals posted as 'missing' sometimes remained so well into the following year, when the front line was many miles away. The simple loss of an identifying label meant the difference between a marked grave and a name inscribed at Thiepval, where Second Lieutenant Hadley is remembered. It is sobering to think that there are 2,480 unidentified burials in Ovillers Military Cemetery alone, over 1,000 at Gordon Dump Cemetery, and

28   *The Weston Mercury & Somerset Gazette* newspaper, 29 July 1916.
29   The 'marshy ground' suggests the officer fell in the hollow of Mash Valley, close to the Y Sap crater, before it rises towards the northern edge of La Boisselle.
30   TNA WO339/43077: 2/Lt. CV Hadley service record.
31   Ibid.
32   Ibid.

1,380 at Pozières British Cemetery – the three largest and closest in proximity to La Boisselle itself.

Second Lieutenant Hadley's brother, Geoffrey, who was a lieutenant in the 3rd Birmingham Pals, was taken prisoner in April 1917, and repatriated towards the end of the following year. The stress upon the family at home, grieving one son and anxiously waiting for news of the other, can barely be imagined.

Figure 9.18 The giant arch of the Thiepval Memorial to the Missing of the Somme. It is impossible to gain a perspective of the sheer scale of this monument unless visited in person. (Author's collection)

Second Lieutenant Bernard William Pigg

10th Battalion, Worcestershire Regiment
Killed in action 3 July 1916

A native of Cambridge, Bernard [Figure 9.19] was born on 18 September 1888. His father, Charles, was a university tutor, and his mother's name was Alice (both later lived in Cheltenham, where another son, Charles, attended the town's college). Bernard was a student at Tonbridge School in Kent, becoming its captain in his final year, and he then went on to Jesus College, Cambridge, where he excelled at golf and cricket. In civilian life, he became a broker, but also served with the Honourable Artillery Company, going with them to France in September 1914. Sergeant Pigg was invalided home with frostbite, and received his commission with the Worcestershire Regiment upon recovery, returning to the Western Front during July 1915.

Figure 9.19 Second Lieutenant B.W. Pigg.
(Pam & Ken Linge)

At La Boisselle, Second Lieutenant Pigg was selected to lead B Company in the attack, as his immediate superior had been ordered to stay behind to help rebuild the battalion in the event of heavy officer casualties. (In the case of 10/Worcesters, this proved to be a prophetic decision). Whilst waiting in the trenches prior to the assault, the Worcesters were heavily shelled for a number of hours, and the company sergeant major, F Yeates, DCM, recalled:

> It was during this period that the company saw what a gentleman they had commanding them, for if ever man proved himself a man he did that night. He, and Mr. Hadley, his dear chum, also killed, simply walked up and down the company during the hail of shrapnel, endeavouring to keep the men steady, which I am pleased to say they were successful in doing. At 3:15 the signal came and we were off just like a lot of school-boys and quite as happy, for we were all eager to get to close quarters. We had got to the first German line when a German officer jumped up and shouted in English 'Retire'. Mr. Pigg at once shot him dead and almost at the same moment was shot himself. Mr. Hadley ran towards him, but it was all over.[33]

33 *Worcestershire Regiment Magazine,* January 1950, p. 203.

This particular incident is similar to the one mentioned previously regarding the death of an English officer who raised his revolver at *Offizier Aspirant* Brachat, only to be killed a split second later by a comrade of the latter. However, if Brachat's memory of the event is accurate, then the above occurred during the evening of 2 July – when 58 Brigade was conducting its assault on La Boisselle – and not the early morning of the 3rd, during 57 Brigade's advance. (In the book *Tonbridge School and the Great War of 1914-1919*, published in 1923, a fellow subaltern of Second Lieutenant Pigg's presumed that the German who shouted the word 'Retire!' was actually dressed in the uniform of a British officer, but that is not corroborated in other reports).

Various soldiers in Second Lieutenant Pigg's company witnessed his death, with Private Watch, a stretcher bearer, recalling it was at the hands of a machine gun, whilst others, including his 'runner', Corporal Shepherd, could only state that he was 'killed at La Boisselle'.[34] As testimonies of men in the ranks were not considered to be entirely reliable, the officer was not officially declared to be dead until May 1917.

His company commander mourned his loss and noted he had been 'marked for accelerated promotion', whereas his CO declared him to be '...an excellent officer, quiet, but firm with his platoon; always cool in every situation, and full of common sense'. CSM Yeates described him as being '...loved and respected by all whom he came into contact with. I have never fought under a better soldier and gentleman, for he was both'.[35]

Figure 9.20 Officers and men of 8/Gloucestershire Regiment 1915.
(*Cheltenham Chronicle & Gloucestershire Graphic*)

34   TNA WO339/36472: 2/Lt. BW Pigg service record.
35   Tonbridge School, *Tonbridge School & the Great War* (Uckfield: The Naval & Miltary Press reprint, 2006), p. 260.

Second Lieutenant Pigg is commemorated at Thiepval. 'Bernard completely disappeared with his batman Hancock* and with more than a hundred of his comrades whose bodies were never recovered'.[36] Of the eighteen officers who took part in the attack, nine were killed and a further six wounded. Battalion re-organisation would take some time to co-ordinate. [*Private Thomas Henry Hancock, originally from Bromsgrove].

An article in the *Stroud News* provided its readers with a vivid account of the assault on La Boisselle from the pen of Lieutenant TD Fitzgerald, 8/Glosters, written on 6 July:

GALLANT GLOUCESTERS. HOW THEY STORMED A VILLAGE. MURDEROUS HUN FIRE

We have had little sleep for about ten days. I have had a glut of fighting. It has been my one desire for the last year to go over the parapet and attack. We did, and attacked a village – been talked about in the papers a lot. The Huns were very stubborn and gave us hell, but the village is ours… We had to hang on to the village under a murderous fire. The Regiment managed to consolidate a position half-way through the village, and held it against attacks during the early morning. I went through the village three times, but each time was forced back to the half-way through line … Personally I killed several Huns…but enough of war. The noise of the screaming shrapnel, the whistle of bullets, the rending, tearing explosions of the H.E. [high explosive shells], the excitement, the suspense, the ghastly sights, and want of sleep after a time began to tell on one's nerves and brain… The trenches are quite flooded in liquid mud and water, which now reaches nearly to one's waist.[37]

(Before the month was out, Lieutenant Fitzgerald was dead). By 4 am on 3 July, 10/Worcesters and 8/North Staffords had both gone forward, but within an hour, their bomb supply had run short, so men of 8/Glosters were sent up both as reinforcements, and grenade carriers. At 5 am, news came back that the Worcesters had been held up, and half an hour later, 8/Glosters' bombers were sent to strengthen the left flank which was facing fierce resistance. At 6:20 am, Lieutenant Colonel Carton de Wiart, the CO of 8/Glosters, requested the line was strengthened by 10/Royal Warwicks, which was then holding the British front line in readiness to be called into action when needed. This occurred just before 8 am, and now the entire brigade was committed to the capture of La Boisselle, but with the commanding officers of 10/Worcesters and 8/North Staffords – Lieutenant Colonel Royston-Pigott and Major Wedgwood, DSO – both having been killed early on in the advance, Lieutenant Colonel Carton

36   *Worcestershire Regiment Magazine,* January 1950, p. 203.
37   *Stroud News* newspaper, 21 July 1916.

de Wiart was placed in overall command of the entire fighting force in the village. Lieutenant Colonel Heath, 10/Royal Warwicks, was also wounded when his battalion joined the fray.

Later that morning, the strong German counter-attack which accounted for many British officers and men was launched from the north-east of La Boisselle, pushing the attacking troops back towards the south-western reaches of the hamlet, and the situation became critical. In his autobiography, *Happy Odyssey*, Lieutenant Colonel Carton de Wiart mentions the German ruse of compelling the British to fall back after they shouted 'Retire!' in English to confuse them, and

Figure 9.21 Lieutenant Colonel A.P.G. Carton de Wiart VC. (Author's collection)

gives credit to his own officers for rallying the men before ensuring their task was pursued rigorously to its bloody conclusion. (Already during the Great War, Carton de Wiart had lost an eye and his left hand, which had to be amputated following an explosion. At La Boisselle, he was compelled to pull pins out of grenades with his teeth before using his remaining hand to hurl them at the enemy). As the German surge ploughed onwards, there was a real fear that the position would have to be evacuated, at which point Lieutenant Colonel Carton de Wiart [Figure 9.21] spotted a group of enemy soldiers advancing rapidly down a trench. With only a handful of men at his disposal, the officer dispatched them to block the movement, and the Germans failed to regain a significant footing in the line from that moment. The CO was of the opinion that a battalion commander's place in battle should be where the fighting is at its fiercest, as inexperienced troops often needed a *visible* presence of authority to spur them on at difficult times. He also made a mention of the deep dug-outs which had been captured, and although he had no idea how relatively comfortable and sheltered they were under the circumstances, he was fully aware of their fatal flaws under attack, as numerous British grenades proved.

In *Happy Odyssey*, Lieutenant Colonel Carton de Wiart makes no reference to receiving a Victoria Cross for his actions at La Boisselle. The citation reads:

> For most conspicuous bravery, coolness and determination during severe operations of a prolonged nature. It was owing in great measure to his dauntless courage and inspiring example that a serious reverse was averted. He displayed the utmost energy and courage in forcing our attack home. After three other battalion commanders had become casualties, he controlled their commands, and ensured that the ground won was maintained at all costs. He frequently exposed himself in the organisation of positions and of supplies, passing unflinchingly

through fire barrage of the most intense nature. His gallantry was inspiring to us all.[38]

His association with 8/Glosters was short-lived. Appointed its CO just prior to the Somme offensive, he was wounded at High Wood at the end of July 1916 – where he credits his survival was due solely to his faithful servant, Holmes, who dragged him into a shell-hole under fire and then helped him to a dressing station – and, upon his recovery, he took command of 8/North Staffords. Injured on many occasions, he survived the conflict and served during the Second World War, where he was captured by the Italians. Throughout his impressive military career, which began in 1899, he maintained a healthy respect for officers and men of 8/Glosters, and when he died in 1963, aged eighty-three, three survivors from the fighting at La Boisselle attended a Requiem Mass held in his honour at Westminster Cathedral.

Every officer* of 8/Glosters had become casualties by nightfall on 3 July 1916 – a measure of the 'murderous Hun fire' which was directed upon them during the desperate fighting. [*Killed or wounded – none were posted as 'missing'].

Captain Harleigh Cox
8th Battalion, Gloucestershire Regiment
Killed in action 3 July 1916

Born on 1 January 1892, in Bath, Somerset, he was the son of William – a master bootmaker – and Amelia. Harleigh [Figure 9.22] was educated at King Edward School in the Georgian city before passing the Inter-Bachelor of Law examination in London, said to be a very advanced test of knowledge in that particular chosen field. He then found employment as a solicitor's clerk with Messrs Long and Lavington in Bath, as well as joining the special reserve of the army prior to the war. Harleigh was about to take his final law exam when he was mobilised, spending the early part of the conflict drilling new recruits at Horfield Barracks in Bristol. On 9 July 1915, he married Gladys Morgan in south Wales, and just weeks later he went to France

Figure 9.22 Captain H. Cox (*Bath Herald*)

with his battalion. Private Roberts, of Gloucester, provided the details of his officer's death on 3 July 1916: '[Informant] states that in France we were in the advance on July 1st [he gave the wrong date]. At 7 a.m. in No Man's Land I saw Capt. Cox hit in the arm and then straight through the head. I did not know for certain he was dead until one of our men came back and told me. I got wounded between 8 and 9 a.m.'.[39]

The twenty-four year old is remembered at Thiepval. 'By his death a career of unusual promise and brilliance has been brought to a premature close. [He] was a fine, promising young fellow'.[40]

Captain Elliot Hampden Crooke
8th Battalion, Gloucestershire Regiment
Killed in action 3 July 1916

The second son of William Crooke, of the Indian Civil Service, and Alice, he was born in India on 30 November 1890. Educated at Cheltenham College, Elliot [Figure 9.23] then excelled academically at two of Oxford University's famous colleges, Magdalen and Brasenose, whilst also serving in the Officer Training Corps. He was a journalist when he enlisted into the army on 5 August 1914, just a day after war had been declared. Commissioned into the Gloucestershire Regiment, he went with them to France during July 1915. His adjutant later spoke of his coolness and bravery at all times, and recalled two occasions when Captain Crooke's presence of mind saved many lives.

On 3 July 1916, the officer and five of his comrades were killed by the same high explosive shell as they were advancing towards La Boisselle. The twenty-five year old is commemorated at Thiepval.

Figure 9.23 Captain E.H. Crooke.
(*Cheltenham Chronicle & Gloucestershire Graphic*)

39   TNA WO339/9085: Capt. H Cox service record.
40   *Bath Herald* newspaper, 15 July 1916.

Captain William John Mason
8th Battalion, Gloucestershire Regiment
Killed in action 3 July 1916

> On Thursday [13th July] his parents received a most touching letter of sympathy signed by all his fellow officers. From it, it is gathered that in the great offensive on July 3rd, whilst leading his men, he was killed instantly, so that, at any rate, they have the comfort of knowing he suffered no long agony.[41]

Figure 9.24 Captain W.J. Mason.
(Author's collection)

Another scholar of outstanding promise, William [Figure 9.24] was born in Newington, London, on 19 May 1889. His father, Bowler, was in the Civil Service, and his mother's name was Eliza. The youngster attended St. Olave's Grammar School in Southwark, and graduated from the London School of Economics with first class honours, as well as securing two prestigious prizes whilst there. In 1908 he was appointed an examiner in the Exchequer and Audit Department, and also spent four years with the Civil Service Rifles. By 1914, he was a lecturer in economics at Bristol University, in addition to serving with the local OTC, so a commission with the Glosters was a natural progression (the 8th Battalion had been raised in Bristol during September 1914). In his civilian occupation, it was said of him:

> He was one of the best; and it was a delight to see how step by step he was advancing in knowledge, influence and reputation… The loss at the age of 27 of such a man, a real student of a subject a true knowledge of which is so important at the present juncture [the country was experiencing severe economic problems at the time due to the ongoing conflict] is great, and the unstinted sympathy of a wide circle of friends will be some solace to the bereaved parents.[42]

Captain Mason's name is also to be found on the Thiepval Memorial to the Missing. At a memorial service in his former place of worship at Streatham, a large number of Boy Scouts were in attendance to honour the memory of the man who was instrumental in forming the troop in connection with the church. Three buglers of 6/South London Volunteer Regiment concluded the proceedings with the Last Post.

41   *Streatham News* newspaper, 14 July 1916.
42   Ibid.

Second Lieutenant Edward Jason Evans
9th (attached 8th) Battalion,
Gloucestershire Regiment
Killed in action 3 July 1916

On 29 June, Second Lieutenant Evans wrote a letter to his parents stating he and his battalion were 'doing nothing but waiting'. They were billeted on the edge of a wood in beautiful surroundings, and he remarked how difficult it was to imagine that fierce fighting was raging so near. On 3 July he sent a simple message declaring 'I am well',[43] which he obviously posted just before going into action. In all the communications he had written, the young subaltern had deliberately omitted any details of his time in the trenches, and it was therefore a complete shock to his family when they heard, via telegram, that he had been killed in action, as they believed he was away from the firing line.

Figure 9.25 Second Lieutenant E.J. Evans.
(Pam & Ken Linge)

Born in Leominster, Herefordshire, on 28 September 1890, he was the son of William and Sarah. Edward [Figure 9.25] was educated at Bromyard Grammar School, and he trained at St Paul's College, Cheltenham (not to be confused with Cheltenham College itself, which was entirely separate) to become a teacher. He played cricket and football to a high standard, and joined a Public Schools battalion at the outbreak of war before receiving his commission with the Gloucestershire Regiment in January 1915. The following October he married Agnes Bufton, and he went to France the succeeding month, initially with 9/Glosters. At around the beginning of June 1916, he was home on leave, but it was noted his appearance was that of a man much older than when he had first left on active service.

On 21 July, his father sent a letter to the War Office, and his underlying grief and frustration are palpable: 'I should be much obliged if you would tell me from what source you obtained the information [concerning his son's death] as I at once wrote to the Commanding Officer of the regiment and the reply to me was very unsatisfactory. Namely – that he was seen to fall but this had not absolutely proved his death'.[44] Lieutenant Colonel M Graham replied: 'This information was received officially from

---

43   *Leominster News* newspaper, 14 July 1916.
44   TNA WO339/43948: 2/Lt. EJ Evans service record.

France and states definitely that your son was killed in action on 3rd July… It is hoped that you will quite understand how difficult it is during this active phase of operations, for casualty lists compiled by Commanding Officers in the steam of battle [cannot] be absolutely accurate in every detail'.[45]

Private Leonard Merries, of 'D' Company, 8/Glosters, later recalled: 'Informant states that on 3rd July 1916 at La Boisselle we made an attack – we were reserve to the Brigade and went to reinforce. We got to the German fourth line where we were held up by bombers. I was hit and wounded and Lieut. Evans took my place. He was shot through the head and fell on me dead'.[46]

When news of the officer's death was received at Bromyard Grammar School, the flag was lowered to half-mast in respect. 'He [was] one of the most loyal of my Old Boys',[47] stated the Head Master, Reverend Henwood, MA.

Second Lieutenant Evans' body was originally buried at the north-east end of La Boisselle (an indication of how far he had advanced before he was killed), and the twenty-five year old's grave is now to be found at the Ovillers Military Cemetery.

Second Lieutenant Gilbert Sims Gadney
8th Battalion, Gloucestershire Regiment
Killed in action 3 July 1916

Gilbert [Figure 9.26] was born in Oxford on 8 May 1886, and the family lived over a shop in Cornmarket, where his father, Frank, was a 'robemaker'. His mother's name was Elizabeth. Gilbert attended Magdalen College School, and by 1911 he was employed as an auctioneer's clerk in St Albans, Hertfordshire. In the absence of a surviving service record, his contributions in the army, and how he met his death at La Boisselle, are not forthcoming. He is remembered at his former school in Oxford, and on the Thiepval Memorial.

(Amongst the wounded officers was Lieutenant Manley James, who prevailed upon Lieutenant Colonel Carton de Wiart

Figure 9.26 Second Lieutenant G.S. Gadney. (*Oxford Journal Illustrated*)

to let him accompany the battalion into the attack on La Boisselle, even though the latter would rather he had stayed behind. The CO regretted his decision as Lieutenant

45   Ibid.
46   Ibid.
47   *Leominster News* newspaper, 14 July 1916.

James was so severely wounded, he needed five months of recovery in the UK before returning to France. A captain by 1918, Lieutenant James was awarded a Victoria Cross in March of that year for a series of courageous acts during the German spring offensive, and he was last seen holding back the enemy virtually single-handedly with a machine-gun before being taken prisoner. Badly injured again, he somehow survived the war. The civilian army Lord Kitchener had raised in 1914 may have lacked experience, but it had shown astonishing bravery in abundance by the time of the armistice four years later).

Second Lieutenant Gwilliam Emmanuel Henry Ross
8th Battalion, Gloucestershire Regiment
Killed in action 3 July 1916

Born at Lymington, Hampshire, on 28 November 1891, he later moved to Gloucestershire with his family. His parents' names were William and Annie, but he spent a proportion of his child-hood living with his grandparents in Gloucester, where he attended the local Crypt School. Articled to a city surveyor, Gwilliam [Figure 9.27 – the original very dark image has been 'enhanced', hence the somewhat ghostly image] joined 5/ Glosters soon after war was declared, and travelled with them to France in March 1915. He received his commis-sion with the 8th Battalion the following October, and on 1 June 1916, he married Gladys Berrow, of Charlton Kings near Cheltenham.

After his death in action, his superior, Major Harding, sent a letter of condo-lence to the second lieutenant's parents in Cheltenham, expressing the deep sympathy of the colonel, officers and men of the battalion in their great loss. The twenty-five year old is yet another officer to be commemorated at Thiepval.

Figure 9.27 Second Lieutenant G.E.H. Ross. (*Gloucester Journal*)

Second Lieutenant Frederick James Hawker
8th Battalion, Gloucestershire Regiment
Died of wounds 16 July 1916

The cause of Second Lieutenant Hawker's death was due to 'tetanus and sepsis' [an infection of the blood] following a 'perforated bullet wound left chest [and] bomb wound right arm'.[48] By this time, nearly two weeks after he was struck down in the fighting at La Boisselle, his mother, Sarah, had been granted permission to travel to see her stricken son, but he passed away before she had set off from her home in Cheltenham.

Born in the Gloucestershire town during 1890, he was the son of John, a glass and china dealer. Frederick [Figure 9.28] was educated at Christ Church School, Cheltenham, and then served an apprenticeship in a drapery firm before finding employment at Messrs Jolly and Son, Ltd, a department store retailer in Bath. He was well known in Somerset for his footballing prowess, captaining the Hartley Club as well as turning out for Bath City on numerous occasions.

Having previously served with the Territorials, he enlisted into the ranks of the Worcesters in September 1914, and

Figure 9.28 Second Lieutenant F.J. Hawker (*Bath Herald*)

eagerly sought a commission, which he eventually obtained with the Gloucestershire Regiment. He married Kathleen Lock in December 1915. The fatal wounds he received at La Boisselle leave no doubt as to the perilous and close-quarter nature of the fighting, and he died at the Duchess of Westminster's Hospital (also known as No. 1 Red Cross Hospital) at Le Touquet, on the French Channel coast. The officer lies buried at the nearby Etaples Military Cemetery. (His brother, Lieutenant Albert Hawker, 9/Glosters, also died in France at the age of twenty-six, just a month after the signing of the armistice. Both siblings are remembered on the family gravestone in Cheltenham Cemetery).

When Lieutenant Charles Lander, 10/Royal Warwickshire Regiment, was sent up to the village of La Boisselle during the battle (it is to be remembered that the Germans still held the northern edge of the hamlet at this time), he described his journey:

---

48   TNA WO339/34661: 2/Lt. FJ Hawker service record.

Figure 9.29 The desolate landscape of La Boisselle, photographed in 1917. The chalk around the rim of the 'Lochnagar' Crater can be seen top, left. In the background is Usna Hill. (Copyright: Imperial War Museum Q2772)

We passed a few of our machine gun posts, all standing to, and some rather unpleasant sights as well. One in particular made me feel very sick. I slipped when wading through some water and my hand caught hold of something round and slimy, half submerged, which rolled over and showed itself to be the head of a dead British Tommy, whose lower portions were stuck in the slime or the trench boards.[49]

After finally locating battalion HQ, the lieutenant made his way into La Boisselle itself:

… through the remains of an extraordinary trench system, built during the previous two years of trench warfare by the ever industrious Boche. In all kinds of unexpected places were entrances to dug-outs: very deep and spacious inside, mostly down about 20 steps, with two or three entrances to each, and opening out at the bottom into different compartments with rows of wire beds against each of the walls… No shells could penetrate to such a depth, but they were death traps to those who tarried below when our fellows came over and started to sling bombs down them.[50]

49   Harrison, M (Editor), *Lander's War* (Eastbourne: Menin House, 2010), p. 46.
50   Ibid.

Kirche v. La Boisselle
9. 24. 16.

Figure 9.30 A German pencil sketch of the ruins of La Boisselle church before its total destruction. Note the trench in the foreground. (Author's collection)

As Lieutenant Lander moved closer to the front line, in darkness, he passed the bodies of both British and Germans, surrounded by the debris of war. He eventually located his company which was standing shoulder to shoulder, with fixed bayonets, in a trench which was no more than knee-deep. 'The ground having been won yard by yard and hand-to-hand, fighting with bombs. As night fell they just dug in as best they could on the position gained'.[51] His company commander then informed him they were close to the church. 'I took his word for it. Not a stone remained of the village; it was just a mass of rubble*… My first job was to go round with the [company sergeant major] and dish out a tot of rum to each man – and help to collect spare bandoliers of ammunition off the dead bodies we could find'.[52] [*See Figure 3.5 for a reminder of the pre-war village].

To secure their current location, 10/Royal Warwicks had inevitably suffered a degree of casualties during the previous day. On the evening of 2 July, the battalion was holding the British front line as the rest of 57 Brigade assembled itself in readiness for the attack on La Boisselle, when a heavy German barrage came down upon them, causing a number of casualties, including several who were buried alive. The father of one of the officers who met his death at this time later wrote to the War Office, asking them: 'Can you furnish any particulars as [to] how he met his death?', to which the reply came back: 'No details have been received'.[53]

Second Lieutenant Cyril George Williamson
10th Battalion, Royal Warwickshire Regiment
Killed in action 2 July 1916

Whether Arthur Williamson received the exact details is unknown, but it was customary for fellow officers and comrades of the deceased to convey the circumstances of such a tragedy to a grieving family at home, knowing they would expect the same if anything happened to them.

A native of Wednesbury, Staffordshire, Cyril [Figure 9.31] was born on 14 March 1894, the son of Sarah, and he went on to attend Solihull Grammar

Figure 9.31 Second Lieutenant C.G. Williamson. (*Birmingham Weekly Post*)

51   Ibid. p. 47.
52   Ibid.
53   TNA WO339/36804: 2/Lt. CG Williamson service record.

School, where he served in the OTC. He gained his BSc at Birmingham University in July 1915, and almost immediately joined the army. His family lived at Selly Park Road, Birmingham, and the death was announced in the 22 July edition of the *Birmingham Weekly Post*, noting he was the 'only and treasured son of Mr. and Mrs. Arthur Williamson', and that he 'gave his all for King and Country' at the age of twenty-two. Second Lieutenant Williamson is remembered at Thiepval, suggesting he was either one of those buried alive, or he caught the full blast of an explosion during the German bombardment on 2 July.

Moving on to the attack of 3 July, the war diary of 10/Royal Warwickshires notes that at 8 am, Captain Shaw went up in support of the Gloucesters, with one company on the right and the other on the left in order to assist with the clearance of the enemy from La Boisselle, and between 3 pm and 8:30 pm, the battalion was under the command of Lieutenant Colonel Carton de Wiart, of 8/Glosters.

Captain Henry Lynn Shaw
10th Battalion, Royal Warwickshire Regiment
Killed in action 3 July 1916

Several of the officer's men witnessed his death in action, but, as before, the date on which they thought it occurred differs slightly. Private Workman reckoned it to have been on 'Sunday July 2nd at Albert', whilst Private Broughton believed it was on 1 July '... during an attack on La Boisselle near Albert, about midday Capt. Shaw was killed by a machine gun, shot through the lungs. I was two yards from him at the time. I saw him fall and afterwards saw him dead. He was my Captain'.[54]

Henry [Figure 9.32] was born in Solihull on 5 November 1872, the son of Henry senior and Katherine. He married Grace in 1905, and the couple had four children. Henry became the senior partner in the company of Henry Shaw and Sons, nail manufacturers, of Birmingham, as well as holding a commission in both the volunteers and Territorial force, retiring

Figure 9.32 Captain H.L. Shaw
(*Birmingham Weekly Post*)

---

54   TNA WO339/20769: Capt. HL Shaw service record.

with the rank of captain a few years prior to the outbreak of war. In July 1914, he was elected to the city council, but after being recalled from the army reserve shortly afterwards, he could not fulfill his role as a councillor.

According to the *Birmingham Weekly Post,* had he lived, Captain Shaw would have received a promotion to major. His commanding officer, Lieutenant Colonel Heath, who was injured at La Boisselle, apparently told Captain Shaw's wife that the latter had been 'dangerously wounded', to which she replied 'Can you tell me anything further?'.[55] From other reports, however, it seems likely the forty-three year old officer was killed instantly, and his body now lies at the Bapaume Post Military Cemetery, on the outskirts of Albert.

(In mid-July 1916, the *Birmingham Weekly Post* urged its readers to send in photographs of wounded or fallen relatives so that 'we may be able to place them before the public, who will undoubtedly yield them their tribute of honour and gratitude'. The images appeared under the headline 'Men Who Have Bled For Their Motherland').

Captain Geoffrey Richard Heard, LRCP (Lon), MRCS (Eng)
Royal Army Medical Corps (attached 10th Battalion, Royal Warwickshire Regiment)
Died of wounds 3 July 1916

An inevitable consequence of tending to the wounded close to the firing line was, of course, that bullets and bombs were not selective in who they struck down. Captain Heard and his colleague, Captain CW John, had set up an aid post in one of the trenches as the fighting continued nearby, and the former was tending to a wounded comrade when a shrapnel shell burst in the vicinity. Captain Heard was hit in the back with a piece of razor sharp metal, perforating his lung, and although Captain John was able to revive him briefly, he died later in one of his own medical facilities. (On this date, Lieutenant Lander noted in his diary: 'We learnt....that our doctor, Capt. Herd [sic] had been killed outside his aid post'.[56]

Figure 9.33 Captain G.R. Heard.
(London Hospital Archives)

55 Ibid.
56 Harrison, *Lander's War,* p. 45.

Geoffrey Heard [Figure 9.33] was born at Stoke Damerel, near Devonport, Devon, during 1896, the son of Richard and Annie. He was educated at Plymouth College, where he played for the cricket XI [Figure 9.34], then went on to study medicine in London from 1903 until 1909. Appointed as a house surgeon at Newark Hospital for two years, a bout of ill-health laid him low before he became a ship's surgeon, sailing to Rangoon on the SS *Herefordshire*. A position in Essex followed until he offered his medical services to the army in December 1914. Recalling Captain Heard's devotion to duty, his colleague, Captain TI Bennett, stated:

> On many occasions … [he] has faced risks, which a less disinterested man would have avoided, and his constant bravery was equalled by his constant good fellow-ship which endeared him to all who met him. The risks he ran were never the result of recklessness, but I have often known him volunteer for dangerous enter-prises where his steadiness and skill were of the utmost value.[57]

Married to a Miss Carling for only a matter of weeks, Captain Heard was aged thirty when he died, and his grave is to be found at the Bapaume Post Military Cemetery, near Albert.

Figure 9.34 G. Heard in centre. (Plymouth College)

Second Lieutenant Esmond Hallewell Rogers
10th Battalion, Royal Warwickshire Regiment
Killed in action 3 July 1916

Esmond's father, Sir Hallewell Rogers, was the chairman of the Birmingham Small Arms Company (BSA), as well as the city's Lord Mayor (1904), a Conservative MP (1918-20) and a deputy lieutenant of Warwickshire (1925). He was also the honorary colonel of 68 Brigade, Royal Field Artillery, from 1913. His only son, Esmond [Figure 9.35], was born during 1891 at King's Norton, to the south of Birmingham, and he attended various schools in the Midlands before finishing his studies at Caius College, Cambridge. He played golf and cricket, captaining his college XI in 1913, and on several occasions he turned out for Warwickshire's 2nd

---

XI. Commissioned in January 1915, he fell at La Boisselle on 3 July 1916, at the age of twenty-five. He has no known grave, and is commemorated at Thiepval.

On 4 July, at 8:30 am, another attack was launched with the intention of dislodging the remnants of the German garrison who were clinging on to the northern extremities of La Boisselle. 56 Brigade's assault is described shortly, but there is one officer of 10/Royal Warwicks whose death is recorded as having occurred on this date in all of the casualty rolls and newspapers, but is not actually mentioned in the war diary, so his exact fate is open to question.

Figure 9.35 Second Lieutenant E. Rogers (*Birmingham Weekly Post*)

Captain Charles Edward Coursolles Jones
10th Battalion, Royal Warwickshire Regiment
Killed in action 4 July 1916

Clifton College in Bristol gives Charles' date of birth as 5 October 1878, and at this time (between 1877-9) his future commander-in-chief, Douglas Haig, was a pupil here. Charles' father was Major Charles Jones, of the Royal Artillery, and his mother's name was Mary. Born in Brighton, Charles and his family lived in Newcastle-upon-Tyne and Guildford, and after the youngster's schooling in Bristol he studied at Merton College, Oxford. He joined the militia during the Boer War (1899–1902), and was later commissioned into 4/Royal Warwickshires. Charles then became an employee with the firm Allen, Harvey and Ross, situated in London's Cornhill. (In the 1911 census, Charles Jones is recorded as a 'clerk, billbroker's'), living in Berkshire, and he married Margaret (also known as Margery) Garrett during the same year.

The *Reading Observer* announced in mid-July that Captain CEC Jones, whose mother lived at Pangbourne (his father was deceased by this time) had been killed in action at La Boisselle on 4 July. 10/Royal Warwicks had been in support of a bombing attack by the South Lancashire Regiment on that date, and the battalion war diary of the former states: 'The day was spent in consolidating our gains and the line was held at all costs'.[58] According to the *Soldiers Died In The Great War* CD-Rom, no men in the ranks of 10/Royal Warwicks were killed in action on 4 July, although a small number died of wounds (presumably received on the 3rd), whilst a Private Green lost his life on the 5th.

Captain Jones is remembered at Thiepval.

58   TNA WO95/2085: 10/Royal Warwicks. Regt. War Diary.

According to Lieutenant Lander, as dawn broke on 5* July, the officer and his men in the shallow trench near La Boisselle church suddenly realised that the Germans were no more than ten yards away in some places, dashing across gaps in their broken trenches, and one (who it was believed had been listening to the British voices all night in the hope of gaining vital information) was seen to wriggle away from the Royal Warwickshires not five yards in front of them. As he dived behind a mound of earth a Mills grenade followed him. [*This date, from his original diary, may be an error – see below].

From his vantage point, Lieutenant Lander could see the village of Ovillers, on his left, and as he returned down the communication trench later that day, he could see:

> … hundreds of bodies hung up on our own barbed wire [at the foot of Mash Valley]. I do not believe any of our troops had got beyond for when the attack started the Boche was just waiting ready and mowed them down with M.G. fire. We learnt later that when the mine [Y Sap] went up, the Boche was first to man the crater, he had just been waiting and knew the exact time of the attack, so all our secret preparations had been in vain.[59]

The officer's memory of the final ejection of the enemy from La Boisselle itself is open to question. Whilst Lieutenant Lander claims to have been in a trench near the church on the morning of 5 July, with the Germans a matter of yards away, the official history of the 19th Division states that by 3 pm on the *4th*, virtually the whole of the village was in British hands. (By 10 am, a group of ruined houses at the northern end had been cleared at the point of the bayonet, and this had proved hazardous as a trench on the northern edge was still heavily manned by the Germans, who also had machine-gunners waiting in shell-holes. These were systematically driven back, and although enemy gunners still swept the ground to the north-east, their positions were said to be well beyond the limits of the hamlet itself).

Writing his memoirs during the 1930s from diaries and notes he had kept at the time, Lieutenant Lander may have been mistaken with his dates, as it is more likely he went up to the captured position near the church on the evening of *3* July, as contemporary reports seem to agree this was where the British line had established itself after the day's heavy fighting. His observations of the Germans nearby would have been more consistent with events of the following day, when the concerted attack pushed forward to the extent of the village, leaving only pockets of resistance. 57 Infantry Brigade's war diary[60] noted that by 3:45 pm on the 4th, the enemy's shell-fire had 'considerably slackened', and no significant German infantry movements had been observed.

---

59   Harrison, *Lander's War*, p. 48.
60   TNA WO95/2083: 57 Brigade War Diary.

Figure 9.36 Sunset over Mash Valley, looking from the direction of La Boisselle.
(Author's collection)

Before moving on from 57 Brigade, mention must be made of C Company, 9/
Essex Regiment, part of the 12th Division which attacked Ovillers in the early hours
of 3 July as the 19th Division assaulted La Boisselle. Advancing under heavy fire
up Mash Valley, C Company veered off course and erroneously entered La Boisselle
from approximately the position of the photograph in Figure 9.36. Its men carried the
German front and support trenches before driving onwards into the village, linking
up with soldiers of the Royal Welch Fusiliers and 8/Glosters. Having captured 177
prisoners, the Essex men were withdrawn by the orders of the 19th Division's senior
officers. The company commander was blamed for the 'mistake', although it was
later decided that the absence of a proportion of the battalion would not have had
any significant impact on the frontal attack on Ovillers, which was totally repulsed
anyway.

Second Lieutenant Ernest Harold Farley
9th Battalion, Essex Regiment
Killed in action 3 July 1916

Originally from North London, born during 1891, the son of Ernest and Barbara, he later moved to Essex with his family. Eye-witness Sergeant Cass, of 9/Essex, said that 'Mr. Farley was a Second Lieutenant and in C Coy. Sgt. Harvey had been wounded at Ovillers on the morning of 3rd July….and was brought in about five days later and told him that Mr. Farley had bandaged him up. He [Second Lieutenant Farley] had then gone on and been killed. Sgt Harvey* has since died of his wounds [on 11 July]'.[61] Other reports all agreed that the officer had gone to the assistance of an injured sergeant and was killed afterwards in the trenches at, variously, 'Oviller' [sic], or 'Ovillers la Boisselle'. When the ground was finally taken, there was no sign of the twenty-five year old's body, so he is now remembered at Thiepval. [*Edwin Harvey, of West Thurrock, Essex].

Figure 9.37 Second Lieutenant C.F. Maxwell. (Armidale School, NSW)

Second Lieutenant Clyde Fairbanks Maxwell [Figure 9.37] was, according to several sources[62] serving with B Company on 3 July, but Private Rice, perhaps in error, thought it was C Company. Wounded in his head early on in the advance, Second Lieutenant Maxwell continued towards his objective, bombing and taking prisoners, before he began to grow weak through loss of blood, causing him to collapse on several occasions. Imbued with an officer's sense of duty, he kept on struggling to lead his men, and then, when they went ahead of him through a hail of bullets, he tried to follow in vain. Mortally injured, it is believed he was bleeding to death when he crawled into a dug-out which was then blown in by a shell. His bravery under such horrific conditions is quite astonishing, and he became one of 12th Divisions's 2,400 casualties by nightfall on 3 July, with

61   TNA WO339/59091: 2/Lt. EH Farley service record.
62   TNA WO339/25444: 2/Lt. CF Maxwell service record.

Figure 9.38 Ovillers Military Cemetery. (Author's collection)

Figure 9.39 A group of German pioneers, c. 1916. (Author's collection)

Ovillers still in German hands. His death was later confirmed to have taken place 'near Boiselle'.

A further two officers of 9/Essex whose companies are not revealed also lost their lives on this date (a third, Captain Henry Peake, was in A Company). Twenty-two year old Lieutenant Edward Bestall was seen to fall mortally wounded near the German trenches at Ovillers, shot through the lungs alongside his orderly, Private Digby. Both men were dragged into a shell-hole by comrades, where the latter succumbed to his wounds at 7:30 am, and the lieutenant at noon. There are no details to hand of the death of Second Lieutenant Walter Noble, who is buried at Ovillers Military Cemetery [Figure 9.38].

Some of the survivors of the 12th Division's attack took shelter in the quarry (marked 'x' on Figure 9.38), situated next to a lane leading up to La Boisselle, until they began their perilous journey back down Mash Valley after dark on 3 July.

The capture of La Boisselle was, of course, a combined operation by three brigades of 19th Division. After the war, Lieutenant Colonel Carton de Wiart VC, was sent a report of the battle to take the village and its strongly defended environs, requesting his criticisms and comments. He wrote back and expressed his dismay that 8/Glosters, which he led into the fight, did not even receive a mention. Sentiment plays no part in the strategy of war. Of primary importance was that the village had been over-run, and 56 Brigade's contribution to this feat of arms, as well as its subsequent endeavours in the open ground between La Boisselle and Contalmaison, are detailed in the next section.

8

56 Brigade

One of 19th Division's machine gun companies had a difficult introduction to the fighting at La Boisselle, as the trenches were unknown to them, and no guides were available to point them to their immediate positions on 2 July. However, during the early hours of the 3rd, its men assisted in the preliminary bombardment by firing along the northern edge of the village prior to the infantry assault at 3:15 am. This line of fire was calculated by '...compass and traversing dials on tripods'.[1] Although their location was bombarded by German shells, no casualties or damage to weaponry was reported, and after La Boisselle had been stormed, the Machine Gun Corps was ordered to pin down the enemy defenders with concentrated bursts of fire-power. On 4 July, two guns were sent up to repel an expected counter-attack, whilst four more were distributed through the hamlet during the evening. The following day, as 56 Brigade went into the assault, it was noted: 'Germans observed moving across gaps in communication trenches towards La Boisselle. Fire was opened and good effect obtained. One of the gaps was afterwards seen to be blocked by nine dead bodies'.[2]

Meanwhile, 94 Field Company of the Royal Engineers had, on 2 July, established an RE dump of stores and essential equipment in the '...large crater in Hun lines'.[3] Two days later, the men spent ten hours building a strong-point under fire. Also on the 4th, its sister unit, 82 Field Company, consolidated the gains made at 'Boisselles' [sic], discovering '... a subterranean system, 50 – 60 [feet] underground ... with large dug-outs [and] barrack rooms, holding 70–80 men'.[4] (Once the whole village was in British hands, the various RE companies were tasked with placing notice-boards at all the newly-captured junctions of trenches to enable swifter movement around the complicated network).

---

1   The National Archives (TNA) WO95/2086: 57/Machine Gun Corps War Diary.
2   Ibid.
3   TNA WO95/2070: 94 Field Company, Royal Engineers, War Diary.
4   TNA WO95/2069: 82 Field Coy, RE, War Diary.

Figure 10.1 A German pencil drawing entitled 'Sappe 9' (location unknown). Saps were used as listening posts, a position to launch a night raid, or simply to harass the enemy. They were also, by their very nature, dangerous places to be once snipers and artillery on the opposite side of no man's land had found their range. (Author's collection)

Following 57 Brigade's heavy losses on 3 July, fresh troops in the form of 56 Brigade were brought up to the new front line. At twilight, 7/South Lancashires sent its bombers forward in La Boisselle, meeting fierce resistance, and the Germans lit a bonfire in order to highlight the silhouettes of the attackers, thus rendering them more vulnerable to snipers. Overnight, a large number of wounded of the ill-fated 1 July attack of the Tyneside Scottish were brought in, many in a pitiful condition.

On the morning of the 4th, the attack was resumed upon the ruins of fortified houses, craters and small trench traverses which were still held by the enemy. One such position, which turned out to be a battalion commander's fortification, took a full two hours to outflank and capture due to the persistent firepower emanating from its depths. At the same time, to the right, B Company of 7/South Lancashires had also advanced using bombs and Lewis guns, but the casualty figures were starting to mount.

Second Lieutenant Oliver Colin Harvey

3rd (attached 7th) Battalion, South Lancashire Regiment
Killed in action 4 July 1916

Born in British Columbia, a province of Canada, on 30 November 1894, he was the son of Oliver and Rhoda. Educated privately, he then studied at the McGill University College near his home, and belonged to several sports clubs in Vancouver. Enlisting early in the war, he obtained his commission during May 1915, fought in France from the following August, and received two mentions in despatches. In relation to his death, Lieutenant RF Johnson, a brother officer, reported: 'I saw him dead at La Boisselle on 4th July. He was killed by [a] machine gun concealed in a ruined house'.[5] Corporal Bates added: 'Lt. Harvey was killed [at] about 10:30 a.m. on July 4th 1916. They were taking La Boisselle and the casualties occurred on the open ground. Lieut. Harvey was shot….and dropped down dead, but they were forced to leave him there, as they had to continue the attack'.[6]

Figure 10.2 Second Lieutenant O.C. Harvey. (Pam & Linge)

Second Lieutenant Harvey [Figure 10.2] was training to be an engineer prior to the war, and was aged twenty-one when he fell. He is remembered at Thiepval.

Second Lieutenant Wilfred Heard Miller

7th Battalion, South Lancashire Regiment
Killed in action 4 July 1916

The battalion war diary states that both Second Lieutenant Harvey and Second Lieutenant Miller, of B Company, were killed early on during the attack, so it can

Figure 10.3 Second Lieutenant W.H. Miller. (Pam & Ken Linge)

5   TNA WO339/2568: 2/Lt. OC Harvey service record.
6   Ibid.

be assumed they each suffered a similar fate as they advanced towards the strongly-held ruins at the northern end of La Boisselle. Wilfred Miller [Figure 10.3] was a native of Liverpool, born on 8 May 1895, the son of Charles – a fish salesman – and Nina. He followed his father into the same business, working as a clerk for Messrs Harley and Miller Ltd, and enlisted as a private into the King's Liverpool Regiment. Wounded at Ypres, he was later commissioned into the South Lancashires, and met his death at the age of twenty-one. His passing was announced in the *Liverpool Post and Mercury,* and the officer is yet another to be commemorated at Thiepval.

A measure of the vast distances travelled by British subjects from the furthest outposts of empire, eager to fight for King and country, can be found in some of the stories of officers in the South Lancashire Regiment. Second Lieutenant Harvey journeyed from the western-most part of Canada, whilst the next individual made his own way from the opposite side of the globe.

Second Lieutenant Rollo Lee Viner
7th Battalion, South Lancashire Regiment
Killed in action 4 July 1916

Rollo Viner was working as a tea planter in his native Ceylon (modern Sri Lanka), and had already served in the exotic-sounding Ceylon Planters Rifle Corps before joining the Honourable Artillery Company in August 1914. His age at the time was given as '25 years and 5 months',[7] which puts his date of birth around March 1889. He was the son of John – a former employee of the Ceylon Survey Department – and Rose, who later lived in the Hammersmith area of London. Rollo was educated at Sywell House Boys School in Rhyl, North Wales, and his medal index card reveals he went to France on 18 September 1914. Commissioned in mid-December of the following year, the next mention of him is found within the details of the death of Lieutenant Hoyle, MC, of the same battalion, who was last seen alive at Ovillers on 1 July 1916, whilst acting as

Figure 10.4 Second Lieutenant R.L. Viner's grave at Ovillers Military Cemetery. (Author's collection)

7   TNA WO339/51716: 2/Lt. RL Viner service record.

a forward observation officer, attached to the 8th Division [see page 69]. Three days later, Second Lieutenant Viner was killed at La Boisselle and his body was buried near where he fell. In 1920, it was exhumed and re-interred at Ovillers Military Cemetery [Figure 10.4]. The evening light was fading when I was there, and Mash Valley looked extraordinarily peaceful.

Second Lieutenant John Harold Ryle Jones
7th Battalion, South Lancashire Regiment
Killed in action 4 July 1916

Fluent in French and German, John spent time living on the continent before taking employment with the Canadian Pacific Railroad. So intent was he to enlist when he heard of the outbreak of war in Europe, he *walked* seventy miles to join the ranks of the Edmonton Fusiliers, sailing back to England as soon as his training was over. When the army became aware of his time spent in the Officer Training Corps of Jesus College, Oxford, he was recommended for a commission in the South Lancashire Regiment.

Born in Widnes, Lancashire, on 14 April 1887, John [Figure 10.5] was the son of the Rev John Jones, MA, who, in 1916, was the vicar of Great Sankey, a

Figure 10.5 Second Lieutenant J.H.R. Jones. (*Warrington Examiner*)

parish in the Cheshire town of Warrington. At university, John had won many cups and trophies for running, shooting, rowing and football, as well as playing rugby for Stockton Heath. Declining to follow a career in the church, he pursued more strenuous activities which better suited his character.

There is no indication as to how he met his death at La Boisselle. At his father's church in mid-July, a memorial service was held for the fallen officer, and the presiding priest (the vicar of a neighbouring parish) retold the story of when six hundred children had recently attended one of his own sermons. He requested all of those who had fathers, brothers or uncles serving in the armed forces to raise their hands, and was astounded at the response – hardly a child did not have one of their near relatives in uniform. Reference was then made to the great sacrifice which countless families were making in the just and righteous cause against Germany.

Rev Jones had initially received the terrible news from a comrade of his son, and, after making anxious enquiries to the War Office, the death was then confirmed. Second Lieutenant Jones' body was not recovered to be identified, so his name can now be found at Thiepval.

As a matter of interest, one of the oldest known combat casualties of the First World War – sixty-eight year old Lieutenant Henry Webber, 7/South Lancashire Regiment – was involved with the capture of La Boisselle before meeting his death at Mametz Wood a few short weeks later. Three of his sons held higher ranks – one a colonel and the other two were majors. Serving as the battalion transport officer, Lieutenant Webber was struck by a fragment of a shell and died of his wounds on 21 July. He had been born in 1849.

The death of the following officer of 7/South Lancashires is reported to have occurred on 5 July, the same date as a costly attack undertaken by 1/Sherwood Foresters (described shortly in this narrative).

Captain John Stuart McClinton
7th Battalion, South Lancashire Regiment
Killed in action 5 July 1916

The son of John and Rosa, he was born in Belfast on 11 September 1887. His father was a seed merchant in the family business, McClinton & Co, of Victoria Street in the city, and, after attending the Royal Belfast Academical Institution (RBAI), John joined its staff. Part of a sporting family, one of his brothers was an Irish rugby international. The circumstances of Captain McClinton's death are not known, and he is commemorated at Thiepval. [Figure 10.6].

Figure 10.6 Captain J.S. McClinton. (RBAI Archive/Pam & Ken Linge)

Lieutenant Cyril Joseph Unsworth
7th Battalion, South Lancashire Regiment
Died of wounds 7 July 1916

On Monday [10th July], Dr. Unsworth, of North Road [St Helens, Lancashire] received a letter from a gentleman resident in Preston, who is unknown to him, enclosing a letter from his son, a member of the [Royal Army Medical Corps], saying that he was sorry that Lt. Cyril Unsworth, of the 7th South Lancashire Regiment, had his legs shattered by a shell, and there was little hope for him. Dr. Unsworth immediately telegraphed the War Office and other military centres to obtain any information with reference to his son, and on Monday night received a telegram from the War Office informing him that Lt. Unsworth was killed in action on the previous Friday [this was 7 July, the official date of his death from wounds received in action]. Lieut. Unsworth was only 18 years old, and was educated at the Great Jesuit Seminary, Stonyhurst College [in Lancashire] where he was studying for the medical profession. For five years he had been a member of the....Officer Training Corps, he joined the army last year [1915] and was given a commission in the 7th South Lancashire Regiment.[8]

Figure 10.7 Lieutenant C.J. Unsworth. (*St Helen's Reporter*)

Cyril [Figure 10.7] was born in St. Helens on 29 August 1897, and his father was a medical practitioner in the town, whilst his mother's name was Ellen. On 6 July 1916, a catholic army chaplain, Rev F Crotty, wrote to Dr Unsworth informing him that his son had been wounded, whereupon almost immediately the latter received *another* communication, this time from the sister in charge of the medical facility where Lieutenant Unsworth had been taken, passing on the tragic news that the eighteen year old officer had succumbed to his injuries. The location of his grave – the Corbie Communal Cemetery Extension, situated between Albert and Amiens – suggests he went into action on 4 July, as the position is some distance from La Boisselle (approximately 23 kilometres, or 14 miles), although, as we have seen, the evacuation system was already an efficient method of transporting the wounded away from the front as quickly as possible, i.e., once they had been retrieved from the battlefield itself, which on many occasions was still under enemy fire. Corbie was a medical centre and the site of numbers 5 and 21 casualty clearing stations from July/August 1915.

Second Lieutenant Roger Marmaduke Laythorpe
3rd (attached 7th) Battalion, South Lancashire Regiment
Died of wounds 8–10 July 1916

The officer's service record indicates that Roger Laythorpe served with both the Bombay Volunteer Rifles and the Lucknow Volunteer Rifles prior to the Great War. It would seem he spent many years in India, and only his year of birth (1887) is revealed. His army papers state that his uncle was a 'Mr. JW Allerton' of Bridlington in Yorkshire, although the Commonwealth War Graves Commission indicates that Second Lieutenant Laythorpe was actually his adopted son. (The spelling of the surname is more likely to be *Allerston,* as there were several family members living

---

8   TNA WO339/40932: Lt. CJ Unsworth service record.

in Bridlington during 1911, including a John W Allerston, born in 1871, who was working as a hairdresser at the time. This was undoubtedly the same individual mentioned previously, as his residence in several sources, including the census, is given as Manor Street). Commissioned into the South Lancashire Regiment on 30 April 1915, little more is known about Second Lieutenant Laythorpe's movements until Private Thorp provided the following testimony:

> Informant states that on Monday July 3rd 1916 [it was more likely to be the 4th] at La Boisselle, he saw 2/Lt. Glaythorp [sic] mortally wounded at 7:30 p.m. and left on the stretcher to die. The doctor said that nothing could be done for him. Informant was also wounded and lay next to 2/Lt. [Laythorpe] and saw three wounds in his side. He heard him [Laythorpe] telling his servant to tell his people that he was done for. He was dying fast when informant left him and was taken back. 2nd Lieut. [Laythorpe] came from Liverpool.[9]

There is no corroborating evidence for this last statement. Returning to Laythorpe's service record, the forms give his date of death as 8 July, whereas the CWGC, plus an obituary in the *Bridlington Chronicle* (published on 21 July 1916) agree it took place on the 10th. (The newspaper does, however, print the officer's name as '*Ronald M. Laythorpe*, 2nd. Lieut., South Lancashire Regiment'). Despite Private Thorp believing that the subaltern was close to death immediately after going into action at La Boisselle, Second Lieutenant Laythorpe survived long enough to be evacuated to Dover, where he died in the Military Hospital. His body was buried at the Dover (St. James) Cemetery, a short distance from the main port, and the funeral was carried out by R Pepper, carpenter and undertaker of the town. He is the only known officer casualty within this book to be buried in the UK.

On 5 July, 10/Royal Warwickshire Regiment was relieved by 1/Sherwood Foresters (Nottinghamshire and Derbyshire Regiment), of the neighbouring 8th Division, and the commanding officer of 7/South Lancashires, Lieutenant Colonel Winser, noted in his own battalion's war diary that this operation was completed without a hitch, due to proper policing of the trenches. In conjunction with part of 56 Brigade, the Sherwood Foresters then attacked at 2 pm, but '... failed to advance beyond the line held by us the previous day and suffered a good many casualties'.[10] The official version from the Sherwood Foresters, however, is very scathing of the entire plan. One company had been ordered to take over a portion of the line near La Boisselle in order to eradicate a small section of the enemy's trenches, but, upon their arrival, the Foresters found no continuous defences actually existed, the situation in the village was obscure, no guides were available, and, most worryingly, the battalion was expected to carry out a large-scale attack without previous reconnaissance or preparation of any description.

9   TNA WO339/5853: 2/Lt. RM Laythorpe service record.
10   TNA WO95/1721: 1/Sherwood Foresters War Diary.

(The actual location of this particular phase of the fighting was close to the Bapaume road, beyond the hamlet ruins).

The network was heavily congested, mainly with men of 57 Brigade (Warwickshires, Glosters, Worcesters, etc) who had been in the thick of the fighting on 3 July. In the absence of a promised reserve of men from 57 Brigade, 1/Sherwood Foresters went forward in columns, consisting of bombers and Lewis gunners, and the centre company was soon held up by a large block of earth, some twelve feet in height, which caused many casualties in an attempt to overcome it. Close-quarter fighting continued into the evening, when it became clear that the heavily defended position could not be dislodged at this moment in time. The battalion was later withdrawn, and strongly-felt doubts as to how wise this deployment was, bearing in mind the Foresters' understandable ignorance of the terrain, along with its almost exclusive participation against a determined enemy, were raised at senior level. 1/Sherwood Foresters' bravery and commitment to the assault was not in question, and it was decreed that its men had fought up to the best standard of its traditions. (The British *Official History* notes that a regiment of Prussian Guard had been sent in to re-capture La Boisselle at the exact moment 1/Sherwood Foresters had gone forward, leaving the British contingent fighting an elite, and numerically superior, force). Officer casualties in particular were high, and there were great difficulties ahead as the battalion was shorn of experienced leaders of men to take it into the next phase of fighting at Contalmaison.

Senior NCOs were also killed or wounded at La Boisselle. Company Sergeant Major Cox, MC, of A Company, fell leading an assault on an enemy strong-point, whilst Sergeant Raynes, the battalion bombing sergeant, was injured when a grenade was thrown at himself and his commanding officer, Lieutenant Colonel Sherbrooke. Raynes caught the bomb and threw it out of the trench, but it exploded and seriously injured his hand and arm. His brave actions undoubtedly saved both their lives.

Figure 10.8 Soldiers of the Prussian Guard leaving Berlin at the beginning of the war.
(Author's collection)

Captain Charles Neville
1st Battalion, Sherwood Foresters
Died of wounds 13 July 1916

Figure 10.9 Captain C. Neville.
(Sherwood Foresters Museum)

A series of telegrams reached the home of James and Sarah Neville in Eastwood, Nottinghamshire, following the fighting at La Boisselle, informing them that their son was dangerously ill due to a gunshot wound to his leg. Permission was granted for them to visit the ailing officer at No 2 Stationary Hospital, Abbeville, several miles from where the River Somme flows into the English Channel on the French coast. The matron of the medical establishment informed Mr Neville: [Your son] 'is very seriously wounded in the right thigh and left hand, and owing to the poison of his wounds is very serious. I hope that in a day or two I might be able to send better news'.[11]

Born at Eastwood on 17 December 1891, Charles Neville [Figure 10.9] trained to be a teacher, and studied at Reading University, where he also joined the Officer Training Corps. In the months prior to the Great War he passed both examinations for his officer's commission, which he received in June 1914 with 3/Sherwood Foresters. Camped in north Wales on 4 August, Second Lieutenant Neville and his regiment were immediately recalled to England, whereupon he spent a brief spell training new recruits before proceeding to France several months later with the 2nd Battalion. Transferred to 1/Sherwood Foresters, he was promoted to lieutenant and then captain during 1915, following the Battle of Loos (September/October), and he duly became C Company's commander. The *Eastwood and Kimberley* Advertiser revealed on 21 July 1916 that Captain 'Chas' Neville had succumbed to his injuries after undergoing an operation to amputate his right leg and left thumb, the cause of death being '...decay of the main artery'. The report went on to say that James Neville, a local councillor in Eastwood, had returned from his son's hospital bed confident that all was progressing satisfactorily, and that the officer had also received a visit from his CO, who thanked him for his services.

It was on 3rd July [the battalion actually went into action on the 5th] that Capt. Neville received his injuries. On that morning, following two days of continuous fighting, he was ordered to take a section of the enemy trench by means of a

11   TNA WO339/12897: Capt. C Neville service record.

bombing party. The attack was carried out successfully with little loss and the position was being consolidated when the enemy sent over heavy shells, and … Capt. Neville received severe wounds, but gallantly stuck to his post …[12]

The twenty-four year old officer lies buried at Abbeville Communal Cemetery. It was said of him:

> Deceased was a young man of aspirations and noble ambitions, evidence of which is established in his brief but brilliant professional career. His worth had been recognised in the army by a second promotion in the present campaign, and in the closing hours of his career he proved that the honour had not been misplaced, for he sacrificed his life to duty. By his death the nation, and the scholastic profession, lost a student of great promise, the family a dutiful son, a brotherly brother and [to] a very wide circle of intimate acquaintances a true friend, whose memory they will honour and cherish as one of the bravest and best.[13]

Upon hearing of his stricken sibling, his brother, George, also requested a pass from the War Office to travel to France, stating: 'We have always been the closest chums'.[14]

Lieutenant Henry Peverell Rogers
1st Battalion, Sherwood Foresters
Killed in action 5 July 1916

Figure 10.10 Inscription on Thiepval Memorial. (Author's collection)

Henry's father, also called Henry, was a captain in the Royal Navy, and took an active part in the suppression of the slave trade, intercepting foreign ships taking its human cargo to the Americas during the 1840s. Upon his retirement, and following the death of his first wife, he married Eugenia Shortland, fathering six children, including Henry Peverell Rogers, born in the Plymouth area on 12 October 1896. Young Henry was educated at Blundell's School, Devon, from 1909 until 1914 (during which period his eighty-eight year old father passed away), and he became a second lieutenant with the Sherwood Foresters in April 1915. He joined up with the 1st Battalion in

---

12   *Eastwood & Kimberley Advertiser* newspaper, 21 July 1916.
13   Ibid.
14   TNA WO339/12897: Capt. C Neville service record.

mid-June 1916, by which time he was a full lieutenant. Another whose final moments are not documented, his death was reported in several West Country newspapers stating simply he had been 'killed in action'. Lieutenant Rogers has no known grave, and is remembered at Thiepval [Figure 10.10 – author's collection].

Before the end of the year, two of his siblings were also dead. Private Frederick Rogers, of 12/Royal Fusiliers, was killed in action near the Somme's Delville Wood on 3 September, whilst Major Edward Rogers, MC, died of wounds at Doullens, to the north-east of La Boisselle, on 8 December. The latter was thirty-four; Frederick was twenty-four, and Henry just nineteen.

Lieutenant Percy Newbery Cooper
1st Battalion, Sherwood Foresters
Died of wounds 6 July 1916

Figure 10.11 Lieutenant P. N. Cooper.
(Sherwood Foresters Museum)

Born on 29 October 1894, at Finsbury, north London, he later moved to Nottingham with his parents, Joseph and Florence. Educated at the local High School, he was employed as a 'ware-houseman' when he enlisted into the ranks of the King's Royal Rifle Corps in September 1914, and was commissioned into the Sherwood Foresters at the end of January 1915. He was appointed the Lewis Gun officer of the 1st Battalion during April 1916, having recently been promoted to lieutenant, and was serving with A Company during the assault at La Boisselle. It is possible he was injured at the same time as CSM Cox, MC, who fell whilst attacking an enemy strong-point, and the officer [Figure 10.11] was taken to No 5 casualty clearing station at Corbie, to the south-west of Albert, where he died on 6 July, aged twenty-one. His body was buried at Corbie Communal Cemetery Extension, close to that of Lieutenant Cyril Unsworth, of 7/South Lancashires, who succumbed to his injuries the following day.

Second Lieutenant Henry Westbury Sargent
1st Battalion, Sherwood Foresters
Died of wounds 6 July 1916

The officer expired at 57 Field Ambulance and was buried at Albert Communal Cemetery Extension. Born at Walton-on-Thames on 31 March 1895, he was the son of Henry and Ann, who later moved to Fritchley in Derbyshire. Henry junior

Figure 10.12 German soldiers rest in the ruins. By 5 July 1916, their tenure over
the village of La Boisselle had ended. (Author's collection)

was educated at Berkhamsted and Derby Schools, and was working as a clerk for
the railways when he joined the Royal Fusiliers in December 1914. Commissioned
the following May, he went to France twelve months later, and was assigned to 1/
Sherwood Foresters in early June 1916. His death was reported in several Derby
newspapers.

Second Lieutenant Sydney Percival Baron
1st Battalion, Sherwood Foresters
Killed in action 5 July 1916

Another Old Berkhamstedian, although several years older than Henry Sargent,
Sydney was born on 12 May 1888, in Kent. His father, John, later lived at Hayward's
Heath in Sussex. He spent time as a rancher in Canada, as well as the more sedate
occupation of fruit growing in the UK, prior to enlisting into the Royal Sussex
Regiment in January 1915. Commissioned later that year, he joined up with 1/
Sherwood Foresters several days before Second Lieutenant Sargent. Once again, no
details relating to Second Lieutenant Baron's death are to hand, and he is remembered
at Thiepval.

Second Lieutenant Francis Joseph Michael Shaw
1st Battalion, Sherwood Foresters
Killed in action 5 July 1916

> My dear Mr. Shaw, I am very deeply grieved indeed, that, owing to circumstances, I have to be the one to convey news which will cause much grief in the home of a brother clergyman, and only wish it were otherwise. To the deep regret of all of us here, your son, Second Lieut. F.J.M. Shaw, has been killed in action. Yesterday (July 5th) at 2 p.m., it came to the turn of [censored by the War Office, which blanked out 'Sherwood Foresters'] to charge in the great offensive between the two now famous rivers [the Somme and Ancre], and your son was among those who fell. His fellow officers tell me that he was one of the bravest of the brave, and died nobly as a soldier. But the shock will be none the less severe to the loved ones left behind, and it may be some small consolation to you to know that he died instantly, without suffering, and that you have the deep sympathy of the whole battalion in which he was so deservedly popular.[15]

These words, written by the chaplain of 24 Brigade, were accompanied by an apology for the note being 'hastily written in pencil', as its author had 'other sad letters' to send due to the battalion losing heavily in the recent action. Its tone suggests that Second Lieutenant Shaw, who, along with Second Lieutenant Sargent, was in A Company, was either shot dead by a sniper, or took the full blast of an explosion. Born near Tiverton, Devon, on 3 October 1892, he was the son of Rev Marmaduke Shaw, a clerk in holy orders, and, by 1916, the vicar of Withycombe Raleigh in Exmouth. Francis [Figure 10.13] attended Kelly's College, in his home county, before studying law at the University of London. He was an articled clerk at a firm of solicitors in Newcastle-upon-Tyne by 1914, and gave up his civilian occupation to enlist in one of the Public Schools battalions of the Royal Fusiliers. This was in September 1914,

Figure 10.13 Second Lieutenant F.J.M. Shaw. (*Exmouth Journal*)

15   *Exmouth Journal* newspaper, 15 July 1916.

and just a month later he was training to become an officer at Sandhurst. The following April, he joined the Sherwood Foresters, and proceeded to France in December 1915. The twenty-two year old's body was subsequently lost in the melee of La Boisselle, and his name is inscribed at Thiepval. 'He was a fine lad, and one to be justly proud of, and you will be prouder than ever of him now'.[16]

Second Lieutenant Frank William Burt
1st Battalion, Sherwood Foresters
Killed in action 5 July 1916

On the eve of his departure to the front (2 May 1916), Second Lieutenant Burt made a will, leaving everything to his parents, Frank and Annie. Born on 17 August 1895, he attended Southampton Grammar School, as well as the university in the same town, where he studied engineering. By this time, his father was a manager at the local shipping offices. Following his education, he spent some time in Canada, and a holiday back in England coincided with the opening months of the war, prompting him to join a cyclist battalion of the Hampshires before receiving his commission in April 1915. Just two days after making his will, he joined up with 1/Sherwood Foresters in France.

His death in action, at the age of twenty, was received with profound regret in the Shirley district of Southampton, where the officer and his parents had lived for a number of years. Second Lieutenant Burt's body lies buried at the London Cemetery and Extension near Longueval [see Figure 10.14].

On 6 July, having been withdrawn, 1/Sherwood Foresters was congratulated for its endeavours, and were then soon back in the fray with their own division, attacking the environs of Contalmaison, on the 7th. So ended the briefest and one of the bloodiest contributions to 19th Division's seizure and subsequent consolidation of captured enemy defences at La Boisselle.

Apart from 7/South Lancashires, and 1/Sherwood Foresters (drafted in from another division), the rest of 56 Brigade fought on the southern fringes of La Boisselle, or indeed well into the open countryside to the south-east. Here, the network of German defences was not so concentrated or compact, but they were stubbornly-held and vigorously defended nonetheless, as they had been within the village itself. Some of the dates here also overlap, although the progress of the fighting, once the ruins of La Boisselle had been secured, is in a broadly chronological sequence.

7/East Lancashires had already taken part in a successful bombing attack on the Heligoland Redoubt (close to the Lochnagar Crater) during 2 July. At 2 pm on the 5th, the battalion advanced once again, following a bombardment of the enemy's trenches of one hour's duration, and although partial gains were made, a misunderstanding in one sector led to some of the men retiring under heavy machine-gun fire.

16   Ibid.

Figure 10.14 German map delineating one of the two rivers – the Ancre – mentioned by the chaplain of 24 Brigade in his letter to Second Lieutenant Shaw's father on 6 July. The main waterway – the Somme – is to the south. Albert is to the bottom, left, and the straight road leading to Bapaume is clearly visible. 'La Boiselle' is the first village in its path, followed by Pozières. Note the topography of the surrounding landscape. Contalmaison is to the south-east of the hamlet, and Longueval is at the bottom centre. (Author's collection)

Figure 10.15 Sausage Valley, taken from the Lochnagar Crater, looking north-eastwards. 56 Brigade launched some of its attacks from this captured position. Gordon Dump Cemetery is in the middle distance, centre. La Boisselle is on the camera's left. (Author's collection)

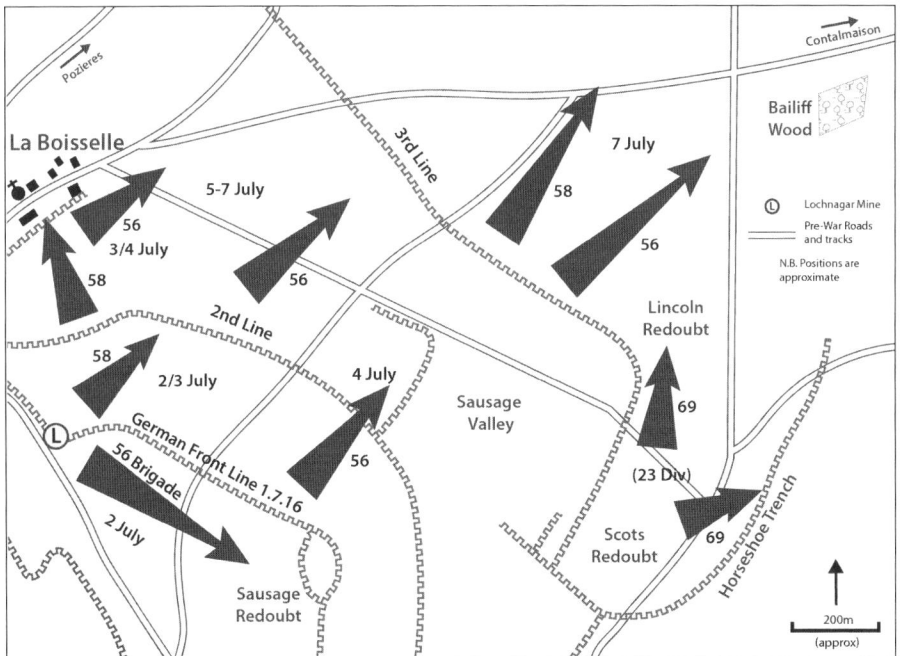

Figure 10.16 The fighting to the east of La Boisselle: 1 – 8 July 1916.

This led to a swift intervention by 7/Loyal North Lancashires, whose participation is described shortly. Meanwhile, the East Lancashires had recorded heavy losses.

Major George Beaumont Tyser
7th Battalion, East Lancashire Regiment
Killed in action 5 July 1916

The Stock Exchange Memorial simply states that Major Tyser [Figure 10.17] lost his life at the head of his men at La Boisselle. Born on 5 May 1877, the son of George and Annie, he attended Harrow and then the Camborne School of Mining in Cornwall. The latter vocation seems at odds with his previous life at one of England's most exclusive public schools, and his future occupation at London's Stock Exchange. From exam results he can best be described as an average student, and did not, apparently, keep in touch with his class mates after he left the West Country, as there is a regular list in the college's monthly magazine designed for such correspondence, absent his name. His details do not even appear on the Mining School's original Great War plaque, probably drawn up during 1919, which lists sixty-three former students who had lost their lives since 1914. He does, however, feature in an amended compilation of 1920 which added a further seven individuals with known associations to the establishment whose names had subsequently been put forward.

He served with 51 Imperial Yeomanry of Lord Paget's Horse during the Boer War, attached to Lord Methuen's staff as a lance bearer, and, upon his return to London, he married Lucy. A member of the Stock Exchange for a number of years, he worked for the firm Robinson and Glyn, and was commissioned into the East Lancashire Regiment at the outbreak of war. His previous military experience saw him rise through the ranks to major, and he was with A Company on 5 July 1916, one of the senior officers leading his men into battle. The thirty-nine year old's body was buried at the Bapaume Post Military Cemetery, between Albert and La Boisselle.

Figure 10.17 Major G.B. Tyser.
(The Naval & Military Press Ltd)

Lieutenant William Lowe
7th Battalion, East Lancashire Regiment
Killed in action 5 July 1916

The original location of Lieutenant Lowe's grave was '…about 240 yards east of La Boisselle Church',[17] and his body was later re-interred at the Gordon Dump Cemetery, a short distance away. Born at Westhoughton, in the Bolton area of Lancashire, on 15 December 1890, he was the son of Robert and Ann. Whilst studying at Manchester University, he joined the Officer Training Corps and became highly qualified in shooting competitions. Desiring to become a teacher, he enlisted instead on 9 August 1914, and was soon commissioned into the East Lancashires. Once, on outpost duty on the Western Front, two of his fellow officers were killed by snipers, and he had several other narrow escapes. Whilst home on leave in April 1916, he married Esther, and returned to active service shortly afterwards. As with so many of his comrades in this particular phase of the fighting, the last moments of twenty-five year old Lt. Lowe [Figure 10.18] remain unknown.

Figure 10.18 Lieutenant W. Lowe.
(*Bolton Chronicle*)

Second Lieutenant Iorwerth Griffiths
7th Battalion, East Lancashire Regiment
Killed in action 5 July 1916

Born on 1 June 1896, Iorwerth [Figure 10.19] had links with Bootle, near Liverpool, and Llangefni, on the Isle of Anglesey. His father, Edward, was an engineer, and his mother, Martha, hailed from north Wales. He became a student at Bangor University in the autumn of 1914, and left during the summer of the following year, forsaking his pursuit of an agricultural career for life in the army. Yet another product of the OTC, his experience

Figure 10.19 Second Lieutenant I. Griffiths. (Andy Teal)

17   TNA WO339/1041: Lt. W Lowe service record.

was recognised with a commission in the East Lancashires, and he arrived in France during May 1916. His grave was also initially situated '… just north of La Boisselle, N.E. of Albert',[18] but the location was subsequently lost, so he is now commemorated at Thiepval. In Bangor University's hand-written student register, under 'Particulars as to career after leaving College', is the rather poignant single entry: 'Killed in action July 5th 1916'. The officer was aged twenty when he fell.

Second Lieutenant Hugh Maxwell Webster
7th Battalion, East Lancashire Regiment
Killed in action 5 July 1916

Another officer of tender years, this time just eighteen, born near London at Barnet on 27 March 1898, the son of Henry and May. A scholar at Marlborough College [which kindly supplied Figure 10.20] in 1914, he then joined the Honourable Artillery Company and, at the age of just seventeen, went to France in June 1915. Commissioned in February 1916, he met his death on the north-eastern reaches of La Boisselle whilst '… leading a bombing party, and was in the act of firing at a sniper when he was shot through the head by another', according to the archives of his former college. His body was buried in the Bapaume Post Military Cemetery, close to that of Major Tyser of the same battalion.

On 6 July, 7/East Lancashire Regiment was ordered to continue the attack and link up with part of 58 Brigade on their right, with the operation beginning at nightfall. By 6 o'clock on the 7th, one officer was reported missing, presumed killed.

Figure 10.20 Second Lieutenant H.M. Webster. (Marlborough College)

18   TNA WO339/41721: 2/Lt. I Griffiths service record.

Second Lieutenant Hubert Vernon Auchitel Corfield
7th Battalion, East Lancashire Regiment
Killed in action 6 July 1916

A number of newspapers reported that '… the gallant officer was killed in action while leading a bombing party in the German trenches. The Germans massed in the rear, and Lieut. Corfield was seen to fall … but it was impossible to recover his body'.[19] A fellow officer wrote: 'The bombing party was successfully holding the enemy. Corfield was particularly daring and in great spirits, jumping about here and there, throwing grenades hard, and laughing boyishly when one came near him'.[20] Another of his seniors added: 'Corfield was universally loved [and] extraordinarily popular in the whole brigade'.[21]

Born in India on 21 December 1895, he was the son of Rev Egerton Corfield (the vicar of Finchampstead, Berkshire, in 1916) and Ethel. Educated in Ramsgate,

Figure 10.21 Second Lieutenant H.V.A. Corfield. (Author's collection)

Kent, and briefly Emmanuel College, Cambridge, his desire to serve his country led him to receive an officer's commission in the East Lancashires within weeks of taking up a classical scholarship at the world renowned university. His name does not appear in the 1921 book *The War List of the University of Cambridge*, which lists every former student who served during the Great War. Second Lieutenant Corfield [Figure 10.21] was one of four brothers who fought during the conflict (his eldest sibling, Egerton, died of wounds in northern France on 17 June 1917, whilst serving as a second lieutenant in the Royal Artillery).

De Ruvigny's Roll of Honour, published after the war using information supplied by relatives of fallen servicemen, notes that twenty year old Second Lieutenant Hubert Corfield lost his life in action on 7 July whilst at the head of his bombers, leading an assault for the third time. No trace of him was found, and he is remembered at Thiepval.

---

19   *Weston Mercury & Somerset Gazette* newspaper, 29 July 1916.
20   De Ruvigny, Marquis, *Roll of Honour 1914–1918 Vol. III* (Uckfield: The Naval & Military Press Ltd, reprint, 2006), p. 62.
21   Ibid.

On 4 July, 7/Loyal North Lancashire Regiment sent three companies into the environs of La Boisselle, at intervals, to assist with the fighting. 'Lieut. Hughes did very well with Lewis guns. Lieut. Milbourne and the Bombing Sergeant were both killed'.[22]

Lieutenant Cyril Rodyk Hughes
7th Battalion, Loyal North Lancashire Regiment
Killed in action 4 July 1916

Although he receives a mention in the official narrative, his actual death is not recorded. Born on 29 January 1895, information on his early life is scant. His father was Major JO Hughes, and his mother later married a TM Law, of the Burmese police. Cyril himself had links with Burma (or 'Burmah' as it is often written throughout the period), and his brother, Captain CE Hughes, was living there in 1919, when Lieutenant Hughes' medals were forwarded to him. Enlisting into the Inns of Court Officer Training Corps at the outbreak of war, he was later commissioned into the East Lancashire Regiment.

The only testimony comes from a Michael Burke of the battalion's machine gun section, who was injured at La Boisselle: 'Informant states that on Wednesday 5th July [1916] he saw Lieut. Hughes killed'.[23] The date differs from the Commonwealth War Graves Commission and the *Officers Died In The Great War* CD-Rom, but, as we have seen, the accuracy of individuals' memories is often understandably tempered by battle stress and wounds. Aged twenty-one, Second Lieutenant Hughes is commemorated at Thiepval.

Lieutenant Leslie Milbourne
7th Battalion, Loyal North Lancashire Regiment
Died of wounds 10 July 1916

Lieutenant Milbourne [Figure 10.22] received a gunshot wound to his neck at La Boisselle, and was evacuated as far as the 7th Stationary Hospital at Boulogne, on the French coast, before his parents, John and Esther, were informed via telegram he was 'dangerously ill'.[24]

Born on 25 February 1894, at Monkton Green, Lancashire, he attended Manchester Grammar School followed by Manchester University, and he was actually in France, as a civilian, when the Germans invaded Belgium at the beginning of August 1914. Immediately returning home, he joined the Public Schools Battalion of the Royal Fusiliers whilst waiting for his officer's commission, which he received during the early months of 1915. His death at La Boisselle was widely mourned in the Eccles district, and the twenty-two year old officer was buried at Boulogne Eastern Cemetery.

22   TNA WO95/2080: 7/Loyal North Lancs. Regt. War Diary.
23   TNA WO339/2345: Lt. CR Hughes service record.
24   TNA WO339/30108: Lt. L Milbourne service record.

5 July began badly for 7/Loyal North Lancashires, as the aid post had become very overcrowded with wounded soldiers, and no adequate attempt had been made to evacuate them to the nearest advanced dressing stations, leading to an urgent message being sent to the brigadier in order to address this problem. At 2 pm, 7/East Lancashires launched their attack, assisted by bombers of the Loyal North Lancashires, but the left flank of the former retired to its original position an hour later, prompting C Company of the latter to swiftly move across open ground in order to re-take the line. Lieutenant Thomas Wilkinson held up a party of Germans advancing down a trench by training his machine-gun upon them, thus checking a determined rush by the enemy. For this action he was recommended for a Victoria Cross by the commanding officer of 1/Sherwood Foresters. Soon afterwards, Lieutenant Wilkinson was killed as he tried to rescue a wounded man forty yards in front of the British parapet. His was the third VC awarded to men of the 19th Division at La Boisselle in early July 1916.

Figure 10.22
Lieutenant L. Milbourne
(*Eccles & Patricroft Journal*)

Lieutenant Thomas Orde Lawder Wilkinson, VC

7th Battalion, Loyal North Lancashire Regiment
Killed in action 5 July 1916

An eye-witness of the VC recipient's rescue attempt told the authorities afterwards: 'Informant states that he saw Lieut. Wilkinson killed by a bullet through the heart'.[25] For a man whose only previous military experience before the Great War was as a colour sergeant with the OTC of Wellington College, Berkshire, Lieutenant Wilkinson's courage is quite humbling. [Figure 10.23].

Figure 10.23
Lieutenant T.O.L. Wilkinson VC.
(Pam & Kim Linge)

25   TNA WO339/5266: Lt. TOL Wilkinson, VC, service record.

Figure 10.24 Lieutenant Wilkinson performs one of his combined acts of bravery at
La Boisselle on 5 July 1916 which earned him a posthumous Victoria Cross.
(The Naval & Military Press Ltd)

The full citation reads:

> For most conspicuous bravery. During an attack, when a party of another unit was retiring without their machine gun, Lt. Wilkinson rushed forward and, with two of his men, got the gun into action, and held up the enemy until they were relieved. Later, when the advance was checked during a bombing attack, he forced his way forward and found four or five men of different units stopped by a solid block of earth, over which the enemy were throwing bombs. With great pluck and promptness he mounted a machine gun on the top of a parapet and dispersed the enemy bombers. Subsequently he made two most gallant attempts to bring in a wounded man, but in the second attempt he was shot....just before reaching the man. Throughout the day he set a magnificent example of courage and self-sacrifice.[26]

Born at Bridgnorth, Shropshire, on 29 June 1891, he was the son of Thomas and Edith. After his education in England, he emigrated to Canada, and enlisted into the 16th Battalion of the Canadian Expeditionary Force almost as soon as Britain declared war on Germany. Sailing back to the UK, he was later commissioned into the Loyal North Lancashire Regiment. He had just turned twenty-five when he fell in action, and his name is also to be found at Thiepval, beneath that of his fellow officer, Lieutenant CR Hughes.

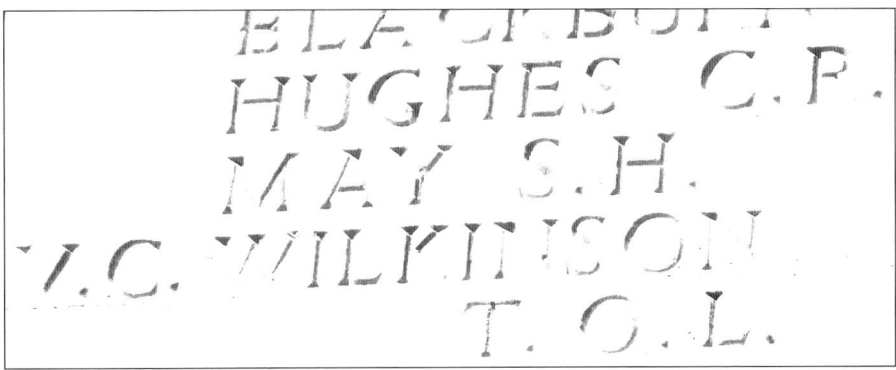

Figure 10.25 Inscription on Thiepval Memorial. (Author's collection)

There was another Victoria Cross awarded for valour under the location 'La Boisselle', also on 5 July, although geographically it was closer to Contalmaison. The 69 Brigade of 23rd Division attacked Horseshoe Trench, to the east of La Boisselle and Sausage Valley, and by late afternoon, despite a vigorous defence, progress had

26 *London Gazette* citation, 26 September 1916.

Figure 10.26 Second Lieutenant Donald Bell leads the attack on the German machine-gun
post at Horseshoe Trench on 5 July 1916. (The Naval & Military Press Ltd)

been made. However, an enemy machine-gun began to enfilade the position held by the Yorkshire Regiment. On his own initiative, Second Lieutenant Donald Bell, along with two men, crept along a communication trench before rushing across the open in full view of the gunners, killing one of the crew with his revolver whilst accounting for the rest with grenades. The weapon was also destroyed, and this courageous act undoubtedly saved many lives. Just days later, Second Lieutenant Bell was killed performing a similar deed at Contalmaison. He was originally buried where he fell, and after the war his body was re-interred at the Gordon Dump Cemetery, to the north-east of La Boisselle. The twenty-five year old was a native of Yorkshire.

On 6 July, 13/Royal Fusiliers (37th Division) arrived in the vicinity of La Boisselle to assist 56 Brigade's assault on German trenches to the east of the hamlet. Moving up into the old enemy front line during the early hours of the 7th, the men went forward to the attack at 8:25 am, with bombing sections covering both flanks. Accompanied by 7/King's Own Royal Lancaster Regiment, of 56 Brigade, the line lost its direction slightly before correcting itself, and opposition encountered was soon overcome. Few casualties were suffered during the advance itself, although once 13/RF attempted to consolidate its new positions, a German artillery bombardment caused a number of problems. This situation continued into the 8th, when a large contingent of the enemy was seen massing in Contalmaison, as if preparing to attack, but a British barrage soon dispersed the threat. The battalion then received orders to push forward, in conjunction with 56 Brigade, although two companies went too far and were punished accordingly. However, several field guns and machine-guns were abandoned by the Germans before 13/Royal Fusiliers was relieved, having also secured approximately two hundred prisoners during the previous two days of operations.

Lieutenant Lionel Bleaden
13th Battalion, Royal Fusiliers
Killed in action 7 July 1916

The lieutenant's date of death various within different sources. The battalion war diary, which was written at the time by available officers in the field, states it occurred on 7 July, and can be considered the most accurate. The official casualty rolls indicate it took place *between* 6 and 9 July, whereas the *Ilford Guardian* believed it had occurred on the 8th '… whilst leading … his men into action after behaving in a most gallant manner in previous successful attacks. He was killed by a large shell and was buried on the battlefield. He was mourned by the whole of the officers'.[27]

A native of Kent, born on 6 September 1886, the son of John and Elizabeth, he later relocated to Ilford in Essex with his family. In civilian life he was the secretary of the British Widow's Assurance Company, and became well-known and highly regarded in the town. Enlisting at the Inns of Court at the beginning of October

---

27   *Ilford Guardian* newspaper, 21 July 1916.

1914, a month later he was appointed to the regular army as a second lieutenant in the Royal Fusiliers, receiving a promotion in January 1916. By this time, he had married Catherine Foley. Lieutenant Bleaden was regarded as a '...very efficient and gallant officer and was greatly respected by his men'.[28]

On 1 July 1916, his brother, Private Leslie Bleaden, was killed in action at Gommecourt on the opening day of the Somme offensive. Lieutenant Lionel Bleaden's grave can be found at the Pozières British Cemetery, to the north-east of Ovillers. To lose two sons within a week is an unimaginable tragedy for their parents back in Essex. An obituary for the latter, known as 'Billy', was placed in the *Ilford Recorder* on 21 July, stating he was the 'beloved husband of Kitty….and son of Mr. and Mrs, John Bleaden…'[29]

On 4 July, men of 7/King's Own Royal Lancaster Regiment attacked La Boisselle with Stokes mortars and rifle grenades, advancing up three communication trenches until they were held up by machine-gun fire from the north-eastern end of the village. On the 7th, it advanced in conjunction with 13/Royal Fusiliers following a British bombardment: 'Then the whole battalion charged across the open and carried the trenches which were the objective. 2nd Lieut. Wigley had been bombing for nine hours on end'.[30]

After establishing itself in the new location, 7/King's Own counted its prisoners, comprising one major, one captain, five lieutenants, one doctor, 400 men in the ranks, three machine-guns and 'considerable war *materiel*'.[31]

Second Lieutenant Joseph Michael Conway
7th Battalion, King's Own Royal Lancaster Regiment
Killed in action 7 July 1916

Born in the Marylebone area of London during 1883, Joseph [Figure 10.27] was the son of John and Elizabeth, and was educated in Belgium, followed by St. Aloysius's College in Highgate. By 1911 he was employed as a metal merchant's clerk, and he was an unmarried man. Initially serving in the ranks of the Artists' Rifles, he went to France in May 1915, and became an officer towards the end of the year. His commanding officer later wrote:

> It is with greatest regret I tell you of your brother's death, he died leading his men to victory. He was shot in the head and died instantly. He was very popular with both officers and men. All his things were sent to his brother as he requested.

28   Ibid.
29   *Ilford Recorder* newspaper, 21 July 1916.
30   TNA WO95/2078: 7/King's Own Royal Lancaster Regt. War Diary.
31   Ibid.

He was buried the same night at La Boisselle, a Roman Catholic Padre did a short service and his grave was marked.[32]

His company sergeant major added: 'He died as a hero. His one thought was for his men, and his platoon misses him very much as he was very popular with the men. As well as serving with him in the Company I was his friend, and he was a Brave and Gallant Gentleman'.[33] His grave was subsequently lost, and he is now remembered at Thiepval.

Once the British had crossed no man's land, and the survivors engaged the Germans at close quarters, the battle for La Boisselle had largely become a bombers' war, with all the gruesome consequences that entailed. The 19th Division history pinpoints two incidents of many worthy of note. The first was that of an un-named officer who was seen walking along the top of a parapet, revolver in hand, protecting his grenade carrying comrades making their way along the trench below. The ultimate fate of the former is not revealed. The second was a bombing duel between two single combatants, who stood in full view of the surrounding fighting, twenty-five yards apart, and hurling bombs at each other until the German was knocked out. It was said that no one interfered with this personal battle, and let them fight it out to a conclusion.

Figure 10.27 Second Lieutenant J.M. Conway. (Pam & Ken Linge)

The final phase of 19th Division's participation in the area was that of repelling counter-attacks, and consolidating the gains made. According to the 19th's commander, Major General Bridges, the success of the entire operation rested upon the efficient disposal of the deep German dugouts, which only the infantry could deal with as the artillery shells were not powerful enough to destroy them. If the attackers had left even one garrison *in situ* and pressed onwards too quickly, they risked being fired upon in the back. If, however, they had spent too long clearing out one particular location, momentum would have been lost, exhaustion may have replaced resilience, and objectives could not have been achieved.

32   *Chiswick Times* newspaper, 21 July 1916.
33   Ibid.

Figure 10.28 A bomb-carrying party progressing towards La Boisselle on 6 July 1916.
(© Imperial War Museum Q780)

57 Brigade was relieved just after midnight on 6 July, 58 Brigade followed suit on the night of 8/9 July, and twenty-four hours later, 56 Brigade also withdrew. The 19th Division was congratulated upon its success by General Rawlinson, who made a special mention of the fine performance of his officers and men. Either side of La Boisselle, the battles, of course, still raged. Contalmaison, to the south-east, fell on 10 July, whilst Ovillers, to the north, did not capitulate until the middle of the month, when the remainder of the stubborn defenders finally succumbed to constant attacks and a lack of reinforcements. There is no doubt that enfilade fire from Ovillers caused many deaths and injuries during the 19th Division's attack on La Boisselle.

In its official history, the 19th Division's overall casualties were put at 3,500 men of all ranks. (A breakdown of the figures, by battalion, is included in the following chapter, and the total is almost exactly the same as the original figures). When Lieutenant Colonel Carton de Wiart VC, sat down to write some orders during the battle for the village on 3 July, he did not initially realise he was sitting on a dead body. After a hot day of intense fighting and combat fatigue, the survivors waited anxiously for the arrival of fresh water. It came up in petrol cans which had not been rinsed first. Sometimes the limits of human endurance are quite staggering.

The *Bristol Times and Mirror*, in line with many other local and national publications, was given information relating to the progress of the Somme offensive from the War Office. For obvious reasons, the latter could not give too much military strategy away, but from the tone of the newspaper headlines, the onus seems to have been on reassuring the British public that all was going to plan: 'ENEMY'S HEAVY CASAULTIES. TROOPS FIGHTING WITH UTMOST GALLANTRY. IMPORTANT TACTICAL POINTS CAPTURED'. There was also a subtle acknowledgement that the Germans were putting up a stout defence and the expected breakthrough would take longer than had been anticipated:

I cannot pretend to present anything approaching even an elementary narrative of the battle. It takes days to collect and piece together, into a coherent whole, the story of such a far-flung struggle. Whilst at the moment the situation looks promising, it is well not to carry satisfaction to the point of too great expectation.[34]

One of the most poignant headlines in the same newspaper reads simply: 'Allies' Losses Slight'. Yet as early as 7 July, the media had begun to realise the enormity of the human cost in rural Picardy: 'BRITISH REGIMENTS PAY THE PRICE. FEARFUL TOLL EXACTED. SUPERB GALLANTRY A NEGATIVE CONSOLATION'.[35] A sad irony of one of the bloodiest battles in human history is that the word 'Somme' translates from a Celtic word meaning 'tranquillity'.

34   *Bristol Times & Mirror* newspaper, 5 July 1916.
35   *Gloucester Citizen* newspaper, 7 July 1916.

Part III

Analysis

9

Aftermath and Casualties

The misgivings and suggestions for future strategy arising from the capture of La Boisselle come not from a modern perspective, but from officers who were actually there. Many are logistical, such as the thorny issue of competent guides to show newly-arrived units the safest way up to the front line – a recurring theme which many battalions experienced. Congestion in the trenches could also have been eased if proper policing had been in force, according to the commanding officer of 7/South Lancashires. Simple signposts would have prevented all manner of groups, including stretcher-bearers, carrying parties and infantry destined for the forward positions, from getting lost. Weaponry such as rifle grenades did not have accompanying cartridges sent up with them, whilst Lewis gun drums were not carried back for refilling, leading to an inevitable shortage. Communication between brigades and battalions systematically broke down under fire, with the only credible solution employing a vulnerable runner to ferry messages back and forth. (Several signalling lamps had been shattered by direct hits at brigade HQ, and telephone wires barely lasted a few minutes under a heavy artillery barrage). On the subject of the actual methods of fighting, the following was put forward:

> I have no suggestions to offer as to how to overcome hostile Machine Guns. So far as my experience goes they had no flanks to get round, i.e., as soon as one tried to get round the flank of one gun, one came under close fire of another. An advance under close fire of a Stokes Mortar appears to me the most feasible, but this takes some time to ascertain where one's own men have got to. We had many casualties caused from our own Stokes Mortar bombs.[1]

On a more positive note, the CO concluded: 'Officers and all my men who did any bombing are unanimous in stating that they could out-throw the enemy by

---

1   The National Archives WO95/2081: 7/South Lancashire Regt. War Diary.

Figure 11.1 The Memorial to the 34th Division, at the north-eastern end of La Boisselle. This monument is easy to miss, as it is situated in a field just beyond the final houses of the village. In the background is the Albert-Bapaume road. (Author's collection)

about 5 yards. This has given them great confidence'.[2] Lieutenant Lander [Figure 11.2], of 10/Royal Warwickshires, had his own opinions: 'The cause of excessive losses amongst officers was the fact that they wore knee breeches and as we afterwards learned from prisoners, were easily discernible by the German snipers'.[3]

The evolution of the British army on the Somme came about via recommendations, modifications and harsh experience which enabled them to adapt and become a battle-hardened fighting unit capable of matching the Germans on the Western Front. Without the knowledge of the fighting in 1916 – horrific as it became – the outcome of the war for General Haig's men, and the world as a whole, may well have been entirely different.

There is no doubt, however, that the taking of La Boisselle was a magnificent achievement, considering the bloodshed

Figure 11.2 Lieutenant Lander. (Tommies Guides)

which had occurred there on 1 July, rendering it apparently invincible in daylight. To then storm its defences and tenaciously hang on, clearing each dug-out and defensive system in turn under a close, sustained and heavy fire, is nothing short of remarkable. The personal and combined bravery, resourcefulness, resilience and sacrifice of the officers featured in this book, plus the men who followed them into combat, are attributes which we, today, should still recognise and acknowledge with pride as time moves on and memories fade. 'This was a soldier's battle, when the determination and grit of the individual comes so prominently to the fore. These qualities were shown to such an extent that the name of the Brigade will remain famous'.[4]

19th Division's Casualties: 1 – 10 July 1916

The following lists are compiled from original war diaries, official histories and casualty rolls, and include the twelve infantry regiments which all suffered varying losses during the capture of La Boisselle, plus the divisional Pioneers (5/South Wales Borderers), and the two battalions which were drafted in from other divisions (1/

2   Ibid.
3   Harrison, M (Editor), *Lander's War* (Eastbourne: Menin House, 2010), p. 48.
4   TNA WO95/2075: 56 Brigade War Diary.

Sherwood Foresters and 13/Royal Fusiliers). (The figures from the contribution of C Company, 9/Essex, on 3 July, have not been added. Their erroneous entry into La Boisselle, when the rest of the battalion attacked neighbouring Ovillers with the 12th Division, would not have featured in the 19th Division's final losses). The officer numbers include (where known) those who died of wounds beyond 10 July, but who were irrefutably present at La Boisselle within the specified dates.

NB: The first list is taken from original battalion war diaries and/or official histories. Those who were classed as 'missing' were not, of course, necessarily dead. If they were still alive, they could either have been taken prisoner, or were still lying on the battlefield, waiting for salvation. In the general confusion after the fighting, an individual may also have made his way back to his own lines but in a neighbouring divisional sector, and then taken a while to rejoin his original unit. The second list, therefore, is taken from the *Soldiers Died In The Great War* (CD-Rom), plus Commonwealth War Graves Commission (CWGC) particulars, and details those known to have been killed in action between 1 and 10 July 1916, along with those who died of wounds between 1 July and 19 July (the latter date was when the 19th Division returned to front line action). There may be a small proportion who succumbed to the injuries they sustained at La Boisselle weeks, or even months, later, but these are almost impossible to pinpoint in such a large casualty roll. Inevitably there will be discrepancies between one source and another along the way, but the figures are as accurate as available data allows, and any errors are entirely mine.

Original Statistics –

Killed, Wounded or Missing at La Boisselle
Key: W/D – War Diary. O/H – Official History. SDGW – *Soldiers Died In The Great War* CD-Rom. N/S – Not Specified.

56 Brigade
7/South Lancashire Regiment
NB The war diary does not give casualty figures for those officers who were wounded, or for the other ranks that were killed, wounded or missing. Therefore the total of wounded officers, & those in the ranks who were wounded or missing, is an *average* of the losses of the three other regular battalions of 56 Brigade.
Officers: Killed – 6. Died of wounds – 2. Wounded – 6 (estimated). Missing – N/S
Other Ranks: K/DoW – 56 (SDGW). W & M – 137 (estimated)
Total dead: 64. Total wounded & missing – 143 (estimated)
Total: 207 (estimated)

7/East Lancashire Regiment
Officers: K – 4. DoW – 0. W – 7. M – 1, presumed killed [2/Lt. Corfield]
Other Ranks: K – 37. W – 89. M – N/S
Total dead: 42. Total wounded: 96
Total: 138 (W/D)

7/Loyal North Lancashire Regiment
Officers: K – 2. DoW – 1. W – 4. M – 0
Other Ranks: K, W & M (combined): 164
Total dead: 3 (officers only). Total killed/wounded/missing – 168
Total: 171 (O/H)

7/King's Own Royal Lancaster Regiment
Officers: K – 1. DoW – 0. W – 8. M – 0
Other Ranks: K – 30. W – 188. M – 15
Total dead: 31. Total wounded & missing: 211
Total: 242 (W/D)

1/Sherwood Foresters (attached from 8th Division)
Officers: K – 4. DoW – 3. W – 7. M – 0
Other Ranks: K – 41. W – 178. M – 3
Total dead: 48. Total wounded & missing: 188
Total: 236 (W/D)

13/Royal Fusiliers (attached from 37th Division)
Officers: K – 1. DoW – 0. W – 4. M – 0
Other Ranks: K – 20. W – 127. M – 13
Total dead: 21. Total wounded & missing: 144
Total: 165 (W/D)

57 Brigade
8/North Staffordshire Regiment
Officers: K – 4. DoW – 0. W – 8. M – 0
Other Ranks: K – 28. W – 210. M – 34
Total dead: 32. Total wounded & missing: 252
Total: 284 (O/H)

10/Worcestershire Regiment
Officers: K – 8. DoW – 1. W – 6. M – 0
Other Ranks: K, W & M (combined): 303
Total dead: (officers only) – 9. Total killed, wounded or missing: 309
Total: 318 (O/H)

8/Gloucestershire Regiment
Officers: K – 6. DoW – 1. W – 14. M – 0
Other Ranks: K, W & M (combined) – 282
Total dead: 7 (officers only). Total killed, wounded or missing: 296
Total: 303 (W/D)

10/Royal Warwickshire Regiment
Officers: K – 4. DoW – 1*. W – 3. M – 0
Other Ranks: K, W & M (combined) – 72
Total dead: (officers only) – 5. Total killed, wounded & missing: 75
Total: 80 (W/D)

[*Captain Heard, RAMC, is officially listed as killed in action, but contemporary reports indicate he died of his wounds later in the day.]

58 Brigade
9/Cheshire Regiment
Officers: K – 3. DoW – 0. W – 10. M – 0
Other Ranks: K – 25. W – 235. M – 34
Total dead: 28. Total wounded & missing: 279
Total: 307 (W/D)

6/Wiltshire Regiment
Officers: K – 3. DoW – 1. W – 5. M – 0
Other Ranks: K – 35. W – 237. M – 35
Total dead: 39. Total wounded & missing: 277
Total: 316 (W/D)

9/Royal Welch Fusiliers
Officers: K – 3. DoW – 0. W – 8. M – 0
Other Ranks: K – 38. W – 153. M – 28
Total dead: 41. Total wounded & missing: 189
Total: 230 (W/D)

9/Welsh Regiment
Officers: K – 2. DoW – 2. W – 8. M – 0
Other Ranks: K – 40. W & M – 248
Total dead: 44. Total wounded & missing: 256
Total: 300 (W/D)

5/South Wales Borderers (Pioneers)
Officers: K – 1. DoW – 0. W – 1. M – 0
Other Ranks: K/D.o.W. – 2. W – 32. M – 0
Total dead: 3. Total wounded & missing: 33
Total: 36

57, 58 & 59 Field Ambulances
(NB It is impossible to collate the exact casualties for the combined Field Ambulance units of the 19th Division, and only those mentioned in the war diaries are listed below.)
Officers: K – 0. DoW – 0. W – 1. M – 0
Other Ranks: K – 2* (shell-fire). DoW – N/S. W – 15. M – N/S
Total dead: 2. Total wounded: 16
Total: 18
[*CWGC figures tally with this figure]

56, 57 & 58 Battalions, Machine Gun Corps
(NB The same criteria applies as before. 58/MGC does not report any casualties during the time period 1–10 July)
Officers: K – 0. DoW – 0. W – 2. M – 0
Other Ranks: K – 6. W – 57. M – 1
Total dead: 6. Total wounded & missing: 60
Total: 66

81, 82 & 94 Field Companies, Royal Engineers
(NB 81 Field Company does not report any casualties in its war diary during the time period 1–10 July. 94 Field Company mentions several of its men suffered from shell-shock & the effects of gas on 9 July, but does not specify a number. The total of the dead is taken from the CWGC.)
Officers: K – 0. DoW – 0. W – 1. M – 0
Other Ranks: K – 2. W – 10. M – N/S
Total dead: 2. Total wounded: 11
Total: 13

86, 87, 88 & 89 Brigades, Royal Field Artillery
(NB For the period 1–6 July 1916, two men in the ranks of 86 Brigade, RFA, were killed & sixteen wounded. 87 Brigade reports one officer wounded on 1 July, but no further casualties are listed. 88 Brigade recorded 'slight casualties in personnel and horses' [TNA WO 95/2067] but does not give a number, so therefore the figures here are also incomplete. According to the Commonwealth War Graves Commission, six men in the ranks of the above combined RFA brigades (and known to be serving with one of them at the time of death) lost their lives between 1 and 10 July 1916.)
Total dead: 6. Total wounded: 17
Total: 23

Overall Total (Killed/Wounded/Died of Wounds/Missing) from War Diaries & Official Histories: 3,503

19th Division Fatalities Utilising a Modern Database

56 Brigade
7/South Lancashire Regiment
Officers: Killed/Died of wounds – 8
Other Ranks: Killed in action – 48. Died of wounds – 8
Total: 64

7/East Lancashire Regiment
Officers: K/DoW – 4
Other Ranks: K – 55. DoW – 7
Total: 66

7/Loyal North Lancashire Regiment
Officers: K/DoW – 3
Other Ranks: K – 29. DoW – 5
Total: 37

7/King's Own Royal Lancaster Regiment
Officers: K/DoW – 1
Other Ranks: K – 33. DoW – 10
Total: 44

1/Sherwood Foresters (attached from 8th Division)
Officers: K/DoW – 7
Other Ranks: [on 5 July 1916] K – 54. DoW [5–7 July] – 5
Total: 66 [NB 1/Sherwood Foresters' participation at La Boisselle began on 5 July and ended in the early hours of 6 July. On 7 July it was back in action near Fricourt with 8th Division]

13/Royal Fusiliers (attached from 37th Division)
Officers: K/DoW – 1
Other Ranks: [between 7 July and 9 July 1916] K – 23. DoW – 3
Total: 27

57 Brigade:
8/North Staffordshire Regiment
Officers: K/DoW – 4
Other Ranks: K – 63. DoW – 19
Total: 86

10/Worcestershire Regiment
Officers: K/DoW – 9

Other Ranks: K – 114. DoW – 14
Total: 137

8/Gloucestershire Regiment
Officers: K/DoW – 7
Other Ranks: K – 85. DoW – 10
Total: 102

10/Royal Warwickshire Regiment
Officers: K/DoW – 5
Other Ranks: K – 44. DoW – 10
Total: 59

58 Brigade
9/Cheshire Regiment
Officers: K/DoW – 3
Other Ranks: K – 63. DoW – 19
Total: 85

6/Wiltshire Regiment
Officers: K/DoW – 4
Other Ranks: K – 71. DoW – 16
Total: 91

9/Royal Welch Fusiliers
Officers: K/DoW – 3
Other Ranks: K – 50. DoW – 8
Total: 61

9/Welsh Regiment
Officers: K/DoW – 4
Other Ranks: K – 43. DoW – 8
Total: 55

5/South Wales Borderers
Officers: K/DoW – 1
Other Ranks: 4. DoW – 3
Total: 8

57, 58 & 59 Field Ambulances* (from incomplete war diary figures, although the number tallies with the CWGC)
Total killed: 2

56, 57 & 58 Battalions, Machine Gun Corps* (from incomplete war diary figures)
Total killed: 6

81, 82 & 94 Field Companies, Royal Engineers* (CWGC figures)
Total killed: 2

86, 87, 88 & 89 Brigades, Royal Field Artillery
Total killed (CWGC figures) known to be serving with one of the four units above at the time of death: 6*

[*The company, battalion or brigade an individual belonged to at the time of his death is not always listed in the casualty rolls, so therefore it is impossible to gain an accurate figure of the dead in the final four units above.]

Overall total (Killed/Died of Wounds): 1,004

There was another British regiment present during the storming of La Boisselle – 18/ Northumberland Fusiliers, the pioneers of the 34th Division. During the week-long bombardment at the end of June, C Company held the Glory Hole; that undulating topography of craters just yards from the German lines which had caused so much death and injury to French and British defenders alike since the autumn of 1914. They remained here until the night of 1 July (and beyond) in order to prevent the attacking waves of infantry from ploughing straight through this insurmountable terrain, and five Military Medals were awarded during this challenging posting – two recognised individuals who took water and supplies up to exposed areas during the barrage.

Figure 11.3 La Boisselle today. To the right of the foreground (unseen) is the Lochnagar Crater. The topography illustrates the steady incline, from left to right, along which the British advanced in early July 1916, reaching a position close to the post-war church steeple by nightfall on the 3rd. (Author's collection)

The rest of 18/Northumberland Fusiliers were brought into the line during the evening of 30 June, when its men were informed that 179 Tunnelling Company RE, had dug a tunnel towards the German lines, and stopped short some two or three feet from the surface. The intention was to break through in the morning, as soon as the infantry had gone over, and construct a new trench into the enemy positions, thus enabling safer movement for the following soldiers. Upon examining the underground passage, however, Lieutenant Nixon was informed that its farthest reaches were, in fact, twelve feet – not two – below the ground, and to commence digging the following day would be ineffective, as it would take too long to complete. A further complication was the potential consequences of the two mines which were about to be blown either side of the Glory Hole, and anyone sheltering inside the man-made structure could well be buried alive from the shock-waves after the explosions. Undaunted, Lieutenant Nixon and his men started work at midnight to ensure their task was feasible, and even then, after bravely enduring the blasts at 7:28 am on 1 July, the new trench was not ready until 10 am.

The majority of 18/Northumberland Fusiliers, composed predominantly of colliery men from Durham and Northumberland itself, waited near Becourt Wood as the Tyneside brigades began their advance, watching their comrades from the north-east of England walk past in perfect order, as if on the parade ground. At 8:30 am, all of the infantry had gone over, and the pioneers began their own journey towards La Boisselle, in preparation to dig more communication trenches, but by now it was clear that the enemy was putting up a fierce resistance. The wounded were coming back in droves, and everywhere became congested. At this point, Lieutenant Henry Coombs brought his platoon into action, but received a fatal wound in the process. He died the following day, and his body lies buried at the Corbie Communal Extension Cemetery.

Meanwhile, Lieutenant Nixon's tunnel was becoming a source of sanctuary for some of the stricken men trying to take cover from the German machine guns, and 18/Northumberland Fusiliers became a carrying party, taking up badly needed bombs and supplies to isolated groups holding out in the front line. One such muster belonged to Sir George McCrea, and his small band of 16/Royal Scots, with the senior officer commenting later how he was nearly moved to tears by the sight of the Northumberland men struggling towards him with water and grenades whilst still under fire.

As La Boisselle was slowly captured over the next two days, the Fusiliers remained in the environs of the village, carrying out similar duties, and, when it had been cleared completely, they set about burying the dead. Private T Wilson, of B Company, recalled how the sight and smell of hundreds of corpses was, understandably, difficult to endure. For six days he and his comrades had been assisting the attack, firstly by the 34th Division, and then the 19th's introduction. Casualty figures for the period include one officer dead (Lieutenant Coombs) and sixteen men in the ranks (two died at the Glory Hole at the end of June, whilst the rest perished during the subsequent infantry assault). Although these numbers would have been attributed to the 34th Division's overall losses, it brings the total British dead at La Boisselle to over 1,000 men from 2 to 10 July.

Figure 11.4 Lieutenant H. Coombs.
(President & Fellows of Corpus
Christi College, Oxford)

Figure 11.5 Lieutenant A.C. Sotheron-
Estcourt. (Gresham School, Norfolk)

Lt. H Coombs 18/Northumberland Fusiliers [Figure 11.4] was mortally wounded at the Glory Hole on 1 July 1916, and died the following day. Lt. AC Sotheron-Estcourt, 8/Glosters, in command of 57 Trench Mortar Battery [Figure 11.5] was awarded a Military Cross at La Boisselle for directing fire upon the enemy from an exposed position whilst under a heavy barrage on 3 and 5 July 1916. The accuracy of his team dispersed several German bombing parties, thus enabling the 19th Division's own grenadiers to renew their assault after being held up. The officer was killed in action during August 1918 whilst serving with the Royal Air Force.

German Losses

It is significant to note that, broadly speaking, one German regiment held La Boisselle during the week-long bombardment, followed by the failure of the 34th Division's attack on 1 July 1916, and the subsequent capitulation to the 19th Division several days later. RIR 110 (*Reserve-Infanterie-Regiment Nr. 110*) was also assisted by neighbouring battalions, as well as reserves sent in from the direction of Pozières, although it bore the brunt of the fighting from 23 June until 3 July. Its ability to withstand such a prolonged and ferocious attack, and initially resist an assault force of considerably superior strength, is a testament to the training, resourcefulness and courage of the men, as well as the superbly constructed defences which enabled them to hold out so defiantly.

There is an interesting entry in the Regimental History of RIR 110 which notes the conduct of British officers and men during the capture of La Boisselle. The former were said to have led their soldiers from the front with considerable dash, but their leadership was observed to be more of an athletic quality rather than being immersed in an entirely military mindset. Opportunities to exploit success were not seized, and, if an officer was killed or wounded, the men following him faltered and did not appear capable of taking the initiative.[5] This scenario was undoubtedly repeated on a number of occasions, but it cannot be indicative of the entire operation, as senior non-commissioned officers would have endeavoured to keep the momentum going in the absence of their officers in other situations. From contemporary reports, men of all ranks showed great initiative during the battle, as did their German counterparts.

(It is, however, a worthy observation of just how crucial the role of the individual officer was during a close-quarter engagement. Lieutenant Colonel Carton de Wiart's presence in the thick of the fighting, for example, inspired those around him at a critical moment, and was recognised with the award of a Victoria Cross. As we have seen, this largely civilian army had to adapt quickly to modern warfare, and the implicit faith which was placed in their superiors' capabilities contributed hugely to the success at La Boisselle. The testimonies of those who witnessed the final moments of their officers speak of unfailing loyalty and devotion to duty under the most extreme circumstances).

The Germans had inevitably suffered casualties during the intensive barrage, and the blowing of the mines at Y Sap and Lochnagar (*Blinddarm* and *Schwaben Höhe* respectively) caused widespread losses. For the survivors, shell-shocked and dazed after seven days of almost incessant shelling, followed by the colossal explosions of the two mines, and then facing a massed infantry assault, the levels of sheer physical endurance and the crushing intensity of combat is quite unimaginable. Unbowed, they stuck to their task of repelling the advance, and the events of 1 July 1916 are now infamous in British military history.

As fresh troops (of the 19th Division) launched their own offensive from 2 July onwards, the exhausted defenders looked desperately to the rear for reinforcements and supplies. Strategic withdrawals were made from trenches which were in danger of being overrun, and the systematic clearance of the deep dugouts and maze of trenches began, despite the deployment of fierce counter-attacks. When the stock of grenades ran out, the Germans were once again driven back, and the remnants of the garrison were either killed or captured before a small group of survivors was withdrawn in the direction of Pozières.

5   Whitehead, R, *The Other Side Of The Wire, Vol. II* (Solihull: Helion & Coy, 2013), p. 306.

Figure 11.6 German troops at La Boisselle, December 1914. (Author's collection)

Figure 11.7 A German trench in 1915. Note the fire step, which was manned during an attack. (Author's collection)

Reserve-Infanterie-Regiment Nr. 110 (23 June – 3 July 1916):
Officers: Killed – 9. Wounded – 12. Missing – 8
Other Ranks: Killed – 184. Wounded – 385. Missing – 491
Total: 1,089[6]

As with the British figures, the 'missing' category was liable to be amended as time went on. By the end of 1916, of the 499 individuals listed above, 170 were found to have been killed or died of wounds, 171 had been taken prisoner, five were injured, and one had returned to his regiment. That still left 156 officers and men unaccounted for, and their fate was left to be established later in the years which followed.

After the British success at La Boisselle, His Majesty King George V sent the following message to General Rawlinson: 'Please convey to the army under your command my sincere congratulations on the results achieved in the recent fighting. I am proud of my troops. None could have fought more bravely'.[7]

General Rawlinson himself penned a separate message: 'Please convey to the 19th Division my best congratulations and hearty thanks for the excellent work done during the last few days. Their determination and gallantry have won for them successes of which they should feel justly proud'.[8]

6   Ibid. p. 326.
7   TNA WO95/2069: 82 Field Company, Royal Engineers, War Diary.
8   Ibid.

10

The Rest of the War

With La Boisselle captured, the urgency of securing the next defensive German line, or strongly-held village, or woodland, continued unabated. If one unit pushed onwards too far, their flanks would become exposed, so a tactical game began, targeting specific locations in order to 'straighten' the advance as well as maintaining momentum. Much has been written about the Somme battles, and the heavy losses incurred. We have already noted the fates of Contalmaison and Ovillers, secured at such cost over the next week, and once they had fallen the village of Pozières, straddling the Albert-Bapaume Road a short distance to the north-east of La Boisselle, was taken on 23 July, although the formidably defended Pozières Ridge beyond took another two weeks to overcome.

After a period of rest and further training, the 19th Division returned to the front line on 19 July, near High Wood, and took part in some heavy fighting. Lieutenant Colonel Carton de Wiart, VC, CO of 8/Glosters, was wounded just prior to an attack, which meant he did not go forward with the rest of the battalion. He had just received a new draft of eight officers, and all were lost in the unsuccessful assault.

On 31 July, 7/King's Own Royal Lancaster Regiment captured a German position and set about consolidating the area at Bazentin, to the east of Pozières. Private Miller was ordered to take an important message to the rear and bring back a reply at all costs, whereupon he set off across an open and exposed section of ground. He was almost immediately shot in the back and the bullet came right through his stomach, but, despite the intense pain, he compressed the wound with his hand, delivered the communication, returned with the answer and promptly collapsed at the feet of his officer, mortally injured [Figure 12.1]. For this act of supreme self-sacrifice, the former paper mill worker and local footballer from a small Lancashire village was awarded a posthumous Victoria Cross.

In early August, boosted by the personal thanks of General Rawlinson, who praised their high and thorough standard of training, the division moved north to Ypres. So the Somme campaign continued without it, through the scorched summer months, past the hellish conditions at High Wood, Delville Wood and others, on into autumn, with the introduction of tanks in mid-September, the

Figure 12.1 Artist's rendering of the mortally injured Private Miller delivering his message.
(Naval & Military Press)

morale-boosting seizures of 1 July targets, and the final, desperate onslaught to push the front forwards a few more yards before the debilitating mud and snow called a halt during November (by which time the 19th Division had returned to the region). Overall casualties had been horrendous – estimated at over 1,300,000 on all sides (British, Empire, French and German), and the line had advanced six miles at its furthest point. The evolution of the British army was well underway, but amid the newly-discovered tactics and fresh proposals to break the stalemate, the situation was still just that – deadlock. Amongst the bravery of all ranks, there were also horrific blunders which sent men needlessly to their deaths for little or no territorial or military gain. It is the latter which remains one of the most resounding historical legacies of the Great War.

In February 1917, the Germans tactically withdrew to an immensely strong and intricately defensive structure known as the Hindenburg Line. In effect, it 'straightened' the enemy side of the Western Front, enabling them to guard its length with fewer troops – a direct consequence of the losses sustained during the Somme campaign of 1916. Thus, the old battlefields were now many miles from the new zone of fighting, and for places like La Boisselle, the colossal task of locating and burying the remains of soldiers which still lay partially or completely hidden under the debris of war could begin in earnest.

During August of this year, the famous Great War painter, Sir William Orpen, spent some time in the vicinity of La Boisselle capturing what he saw on canvas. He had last seen the landscape as a gloomy, desolate place, full of shell holes and mud; but now, it was transformed into a mass of red, white and blue flowers surging skywards as nature reclaimed the desolate landscape. The devastation of the fighting was never far away, of course, and, as he worked, he encountered many burial parties endeavouring to identify, bury, and often *re*-bury the bodies of their unfortunate comrades. Orpen also struck up a friendship with the writer and poet John Masefield, who had been asked to write an account of the Battle of the Somme, with the latter spending a day at different locations, including La Boisselle, before returning to his base at nearby Amiens.

Orpen was also in awe of the 'Great Mine' at La Boisselle – 'Lochnagar Crater' as it is known today. Its approaches were littered with shrapnel and, as he stood precariously at its rim, he noted that the sides were too steep for human access, so steps had been cut into the gradient to enable salvage parties to bury as many of the human remains as they could gather together at the bottom of this enormous chasm [Figure 12.2].

As the year progressed, cautious optimism prevailed amongst the Allies, as several significant victories over the Germans, coupled with the American entry into the war, pointed to a shift in the balance of power, but 1917 ended with the two sides still deadlocked after the pitiless fighting at the Third Battle of Ypres (known more commonly as 'Passchendaele'), which bled the armies of both sides at an alarming rate.

Figure 12.2 Lochnagar Crater. (Author's collection)

By March 1918, following the collapse of the Eastern Front, the Germans transferred tens of thousands of seasoned veterans over to France and Flanders for one last
desperate gamble. The British were severely weakened, and had only just reorganised
many of their regiments and battalions, disbanding or merging a number of the new
army units to cope with the losses. German storm-troopers punched a hole through
the sparse defences, and there is a deep irony in the manner with which the enemy
captured the ground between Bapaume and Albert in a single day, when the British
took four and a half months in 1916 to secure a position several miles short of the
first-named town. This is not to say, however, that the British and empire troops had
lost their spirit to fight. Some battalions literally fought to the last man, and with no
reserves to be deployed, once the initial barricade had been breached, the Germans
often found open ground beyond.

37 Brigade of 12th Division, for example, arrived at La Boisselle on 26 March 1918,
to find the advanced HQ of the 47th Division already there. General Gorringe then
ordered 37 Brigade to counter-attack towards Pozières and establish communication
with neighbouring divisions. The 6/Queen's and 6/Royal West Kents subsequently
moved forwards on either side of the Albert-Bapaume Road, passing through Ovillers
and on into Pozières, which was found to be unoccupied. The German onslaught,
however, soon arrived, and much of the fighting took place in and around Aveluy, to
the north of Albert and to the west of La Boisselle.

At 9 am on 28 March, a strong enemy advance from the direction of Aveluy was
completely repulsed by 5/Royal Berkshires and 9/Royal Fusiliers, inflicting heavy

Figure 12.3 Mash Valley. (Author's collection)

casualties, and the Germans were observed carrying their wounded across the River Ancre and back up the slope towards La Boisselle. This 'slope' was none other than Mash Valley [Figure 12.3. Ovillers Military Cemetery is on the left, and the western-most buildings of Ovillers itself are on the right, behind the trees].

In April, Field Marshal Haig issued his famous 'backs to the wall' speech, when the Allied line was perilously close to breaking completely, but somehow it held. The town of Albert was now in German hands, however, and perhaps in an act of defiance, the statue of the Madonna and Child on top of the basilica – hanging precariously over the streets below – was deliberately destroyed by British artillery. By coincidence, the 19th Division fought in the nearby area of Bapaume during the German spring offensive, suffering nearly 3,800 casualties in the process.

By August 1918, the British were ready to take the offensive once more, and launched the critical Battle of Amiens (approximately sixteen miles to the south-west of Albert) which finally ignited the inexorable pursuit of the Germans on the Western Front. It was no longer a static war, where defence in depth was king; this was a mobile, efficient and competent Allied army, backed up by tanks and aircraft, combining to ruthlessly harass the enemy until its inevitable capitulation.

On 23 August, 13/Royal Welch Fusiliers attacked a line of 2,000 yards between Aveluy and the Albert-Bapaume Road, capturing two field guns, sixteen machine guns, 150 prisoners of war, and 'considerable booty'.[1] Second Lieutenant Robert Davies was killed, five fellow officers wounded, twenty men in the ranks were dead, 117 injured, nineteen missing and three were gassed.[2] The ways of warfare may have

1   The National Archives WO95/2555: 13/Royal Welch Fusiliers War Diary.
2   Ibid.

121, LABOISSELLE, près d'ALBERT (Somme) — Les Entonnoirs
Mine Crater at Laboisselle

Figure 12.4 Y Sap Crater in the early 1920s. Situated in Mash Valley, it has since been filled in. (Author's collection)

been changing, but the casualty lists were not. The extent of the advance was 1,800 yards, and, on the following day, the battalion moved up Mash Valley for the last time, with C Company detailed to 'mop up' Ovillers, which was reported clear of the enemy.

Also on the 24th, 14/RWF attacked towards La Boisselle and Grandcourt, moving across 'craters and strongpoints'[3] at La Boisselle (presumably in the area of the Glory Hole) before meeting opposition. 100 German prisoners were secured after a fire-fight, along with a number of machine-guns, whilst an unsuccessful enemy counter-attack led to thirty more individuals surrendering to the Welshmen. In the afternoon, as their comrades of the 13th Battalion moved towards Ovillers, the 14th reached the crest of the valley at the top of La Boisselle and were targeted by a German machine-gun, firing from the direction of Pozières, forcing them to take cover in a line of shell holes. The fate of this German position is not revealed, but it is to be assumed it was dealt with efficiently, as the brigade's next named location in the war diary is Mametz Wood, several miles away.

La Boisselle was finally freed from the shackles of war. The 'Advance to Victory' – bloody and stubborn as it was – became a triumph of arms which ended with the

3   TNA WO95/2555: 14/Royal Welch Fusiliers War Diary.

armistice on 11 November 1918. It is to be wondered whether any long-term veterans of the 19th Division cast their minds and memories back to the events of early July 1916, above all their other experiences, or maybe it was just one of many actions which, collectively, they were fortunate enough to survive. In the official records of the Great War, from a stark military perspective, this is exactly what it was – just one of many battles. It was labelled as the fight for Albert and its environs, between 1 and 13 July, and under five tactical incidents is written: 'Capture of La Boisselle: 19th Division'.[4] The true story, however, is quite extraordinary.

---

4   James, EA, *A Record Of The Battles & Engagements Of The British Armies in France & Flanders 1914–1918* (Uckfield: The Naval & Military Press Ltd, reprint 1978).

11

Remembering

Within a couple of years of the conclusion of the war (the Peace Treaty of Versailles, signed at the end of June, 1919, dictated Germany's fate at the hands of her victors), British veterans were already re-tracing their steps on the Western Front. Those who had not suffered debilitating body wounds or severe mental afflictions could recall and visit, in specific detail, the locations of particular trenches, battalion headquarters, graves of recently-fallen comrades, and German strong-points which had been stormed at such high cost to life and limb.

The dangerous ordnance of war still littered the landscape, and the threat of unexploded bombs, coupled with unstable gas canisters, was a real and constant hazard, both to the military and civilians alike. As the latter returned to their shattered towns and villages, some set up photographic studios in order to record individual burial sites for the benefit of financially restricted families from the United Kingdom and its empire who would never be able to travel to France and Flanders in person.

One of the first tasks of the almost incomprehensible rebuilding schedule was to ensure pre-war roads were cleared and then reconstructed, thus enabling the transport of timber and brick across the old front lines. The rare photograph [Figure 13.2] was taken in the desolate ruins of La Boisselle, and almost certainly depicts the convergence of the Albert-Bapaume road (left) with the route to Contalmaison (right). This was, therefore, the position of the old civilian cemetery, near the Glory Hole, and is now where one of the memorials to the 34th Division is situated [marked 'X' on Figure 13.3]. It is barely conceivable that the village once looked like this, but to the veterans who returned, this was all they knew. The new, modern hamlet which replaced the barren scene of the conflict and its immediate aftermath was alien to *them,* and became one of the endless paradoxes of the Great War and its legacies.

In 1922, a wind-powered water pump was built in nearby Ovillers, providing a fresh supply for the surrounding district. Its inauguration was attended by British officers and former servicemen who had fought in the neighbourhood. County regiments, towns or cities which had particular affiliations with certain parts of the Western Front struck up civic cross-channel friendships and organised exchanges with newly-emerging French populations in the once deserted battle-zones. One such *Ceremonie*

Figure 13.1 Old trenches near La Boisselle in the early 1920s.
(Gloucestershire Archives D3549/33/2/5)

Figure 13.2 Convergence of Albert - Bapaume Road circa 1919-20.
(Gloucestershire Archives D3549/33/2/5)

Figure 13.3 The same location today (Author's collection)

Figure 13.4 German machine gun-emplacement. (Gloucestershire Archives D3594/33/2/5)

Patriotique during 1925, which ended back in Albert after a trip to the nearby ceme-teries around Ovillers, included representatives of *Les Mutiles, les Infirmieres, et les Medailles Militaires Section d'Albert.*[1]

The graves and burial grounds were also changing, from the original wooden crosses, now cracking and fading under the passing seasons, to the uniform stones of the Imperial War Graves Commission, surrounded by walls and sculptures from the minds of leading architects of the day.

As time went on, the old trenches were filled in, enclosing the debris of conflict within, and nature took over once more. The French, quite understandably, wanted to put the terrible past behind them, rebuilding their lives as well as their bomb-wrecked homes. Former machine-gun emplacements on the Somme, such as the one depicted in Figure 13.4 may well still survive today, albeit under many feet of soil and chalk.

When the Thiepval Memorial to the Missing of the Somme was unveiled during 1932, it could be seen from miles around, including La Boisselle. Vera Brittain, who wrote the celebrated *Testament of Youth*, which recounted the loss of her brother, fiancé and other close friends in action during the Great War, was scathing of Thiepval, claiming it masked the true horrors of battle and instead gave the impression that

1   Gloucestershire Archives, SR37/41323.18GS.

Figure 13.5 Another rare photograph, this time from 1936 – exactly twenty years after the First Battle of the Somme. The village of La Boisselle is on the horizon, with the spire of the new church just visible. Note the lack of trees or vegetation.
(Gloucestershire Archives D3549/33/2/5)

conflict was noble and glorious. At a time in history when the world was beginning a gradual slide into a second global conflict due to the consequences of the first, the raw subject of warfare had never really subsided.

Returning to La Boisselle, there is one location which stands as a tangible memorial to the endeavours and struggles of men on both sides of the divide during the First World War – the 'Lochnagar' Crater, or the *Schwaben Höhe* as the Germans knew it. The result of months of tunnelling, from beneath the British front line, it was blown at 07:28 on 1 July, 1916, just prior to the brave but disastrous infantry assault of the 34th Division. It is nearly 300 feet in circumference and seventy-one feet in depth, and was in danger of being filled in (a fate which did occur at nearby Y Sap) until Richard Dunning secured the land in perpetuity during the late 1970s.

A number of the officers mentioned in this book met their deaths at or near the crater, and its significance as a site of pilgrimage for Great War and history enthusiasts cannot be over-stated. Whilst I was researching this text, I spent some time in and around La Boisselle, gathering photographs and general information, and every time I looked over to the crater, at least one bus-load of visitors was either travelling towards, or away, from its environs. It is an inevitably poignant location – I once described it as the saddest place I know – but it has to represent more than that. It must also be somewhere to pay tribute to the human spirit as it wavered under the most extreme of conditions and bloodshed back in 1916. To simply label it as the heart of an appalling tragedy is doing an immense dis-service to the gallantry of those who fought here.

Figure 13.6 The Lochnagar Crater today, with its Memorial Cross. The image was taken from the direction of La Boisselle. (Author's collection)

In my opinion, it is best visited alone, during the early morning or evening. When I was there, several rabbits were darting about, and my appearance at the crumbling edges sent the mammals scurrying into their shelters dug into the steep sides. One Great War survivor wrote:

> Even the troglodyte lived in a cave on the slope of a hill, and looked downwards, not upwards, onto grass, and water, and copses green. But we modern nonde-scripts burrow like rabbits, and we even have 'runs'. We pop into our holes when danger threatens, and bob out again when all is safe. Neither can we call even these holes our home. Here today, there tomorrow, we have all the faults of the homeless casual.[2]

When you realise just how many souls died in this one small area alone, it is a sobering thought to know that many are still 'missing'; some are probably just beneath your feet.

Every 1 July, a ceremony is held here, beginning, appropriately enough, at 7:28 am, and a lone piper is a reminder of the bagpipes which were used to lead the Tyneside Scottish into battle. Only those with a heart of stone are not moved by this humbling experience. During the 1920s, a veteran observed:

> When the smoke had cleared away from Northern France, leaving the mangled ruins of 4,000 martyred towns and villages visible upon the shell-churned battle-fields, it is natural that England should begin to ask herself 'What is there that I can do in the presence of this tragedy?'…. On the edge of a village is a memorial

---

2   Sibley, WA, *Wycliffe & The War – A School Record* (Gloucester: John Bellows, 1923), p. 327.

Figure 13.7 The Glory Hole today. The jumbled mass of craters has been reclaimed by nature. This image was taken close to the site of the old 'Granathof', which took many lives on both sides between 1914 and 1916. The narrow stretch of no man's land was bypassed by the attacking troops of the 34th Division on 1 July, 1916, and subsequently the 19th Division from 2 July until the capture of La Boisselle. (Author's collection)

of those days which centuries, surely, will not efface – an immense mine crater, into whose depths some of us stood and gazed in the moonlight of last week.[3]

Close by is another less visible, but no less startling remnant of the Great War. As La Boisselle was rebuilt, the cluster of small craters at the Glory Hole remained untouched, situated on private land. With the centenary of the Great War approaching, permission was granted for professional archaeologists to make a detailed study of the area, both above and below ground. Vegetation was cut back, radar mapping undertaken, and tentative digs were started, uncovering old trench systems and tunnels. It is to be remembered that firstly the French, followed by the British, took control of this precarious position around the *Granathof*, with its associated close proximity to the German lines, often only a matter of yards away. Beneath the surface, some of the shafts still remain, remarkably intact after nearly a hundred years of human absence. A number also contain the remains of miners, lost when chambers were blown by the enemy, or roofs collapsed on top of them. It is a thought-provoking and yet fascinating piece of First World War history, hidden from view. Time moves on, and history becomes a matter for those who wish to remember.

3   Gloucestershire Archives, SR37/41323.18GS.

Figure 13.8 An aerial view of the Lochnagar Crater and the south-western tip of La Boisselle. The Glory Hole is situated on the rough ground between the houses and the open fields to the left. The 19th Division attacked the village from both sides (advancing from left to right). Mash Valley lies beyond the houses furthest from the camera. (Photograph courtesy of Jeremy Banning: <www.jeremybanning.co.uk>)

In a few short months a voluntary army, consisting of men [who] were hitherto in the main ignorant of, and largely averse to, war, yet who loved their country so well, who realised the mortal dangers to which she was being subjected, that they counted not their lives dear to them, but went with great readiness [and] turned their backs on most things that many of us greatly value, focused their face on the foe, and did their utmost.[4]

4   *Dean Forest Mercury* newspaper, 21 July 1916.

In August 1916, the *Dean Forest Mercury* published the following descriptive passage entitled 'The Road', written by an anonymous British officer after visiting a military cemetery [See Figure 13.9] created in a French wheat field:

> There lies part of the two years' harvest of death in this part of the line, and in it one can trace easily the regiments that have been here and the length of stay by the inscriptions on the little wooden crosses that mark alike the graves of all ranks. Shoulder to shoulder as they stood in life, so they lie in death. Irish, Scotch, English, Welsh....each country has contributed its quota. It is a piteous but [also] a glorious sight. Is there a nation in the world which could produce such a graveyard? Gathered in from every part of the world, each one has been a living traveller on our road.[5]

Figure 13.9 Post-war grave site. (Author's collection)

5   Ibid. 29 September 1916.

Figure 13.10 The Memorial Cross at the Lochnagar Crater, La Boisselle, late evening.
(Author's collection)

Bibliography

Newspapers & Periodicals

[NB – some of these publications are no longer in circulation, or have been incorporated into other newspaper groups]

Bath Herald
Birmingham Weekly Post
Bolton Chronicle
Bridlington Chronicle
Bristol Times & Mirror
Cambrian News & Welsh Farmers' Gazette
Cheltenham Chronicle & Gloucestershire Graphic
Chiswick Times
Dean Forest Mercury
Dudley Herald
Eastwood & Kimberley Advertiser
Eccles & Patricroft Journal
Evesham Journal
Exmouth Journal
Gloucester Citizen
Gloucester Journal
Hampshire Independent
Ilford Guardian
Ilford Recorder
Illustrated Western Weekly News
Leominster News
Liverpool Post and Mercury
Llanelly Star
London Gazette
London Hospital Gazette
Mid Cumberland & Westmoreland Herald
North Wales Guardian
Oxford Journal Illustrated

Reading Observer
Staffordshire Advertiser
Staffordshire Sentinel
Streatham News
Stroud News
St. Helens Reporter
Warrington Examiner
Western Daily Mercury
Weston Mercury & Somerset Gazette
Weston-super-mare Gazette
Wiltshire Gazette
Wiltshire Telegraph
Wimbledon Borough News

Printed Sources

Banks, Arthur, *A Military Atlas of the First World War,* Barnsley: Leo Cooper, 1975.
Carey, GV, MA, *The War List of the University of Cambridge 1914–1919,* Cambridge: University Press, 1921.
Carton de Wiart, Lt. Gen. Sir A, *Happy Odyssey,* London: Pan Books Ltd, 1955.
Crewe, F, *History of the 8th North Staffords*, Stoke-on-Trent: Hughes & Harber, 1921.
Cuttell, Barry, *One Day On The Somme,* Peterborough: GMS Enterprises, 2007.
—— *148 Days On The Somme,* Peterborough: GMS Enterprises, 2007.
De Ruvigny, Marquis, *Roll of Honour 1914–18,* Uckfield: The Naval & Military Press Ltd, reprint, 2001.
Edmonds, Sir James, *Military Operations France and Belgium 1916 Vol. I*, London: Macmillan, 1932.
Gliddon, Gerald *VCs of the First World War – The Somme,* Stroud: Sutton Publishing Ltd, 1997.
Griffith, Llewelyn Wyn (Editor: Riley, J) *Up To Mametz…and Beyond*, Barnsley: Pen & Sword, 2010.
Harrison, Michael (Editor) *Lander's War,* Eastbourne: Menin House Publishers (Tommies Guides), 2010.
Hoyle, Lt JB, *Some Letters from a Subaltern on the Western Front, July 1915 – June 1916,* Uckfield: The Naval & Military Press Ltd, & London: Imperial War Museum, reprint 2009.
James, Capt. EA, *A Record of the Battles & Engagements of the British Armies in France & Flanders, 1914–1918*, Uckfield: The Naval & Military Press Ltd, reprint 1978.
—— *British Regiments 1914–1918*, Uckfield: The Naval & Military Press Ltd reprint, 1998.
Lewis-Stempel, John, *Six Weeks – The Short & Gallant Life of the British Officer in the First World War*, London: Orion, 2010.

McCarthy, Chris *The Somme – The Day-By-Day Account,* London: Arms & Armour Press, 1993.

Middlebrook, Martin, *The First Day On The Somme – 1 July 1916,* London: Penguin Books, 1984.

Miles, Captain Wilfred, *Military Operations France and Belgium 1916 Vol. II,* London: Macmillan, 1938.

Moore-Bick, Christopher, *Playing The Game – The British Junior Infantry Officer on the Western Front 1914–18,* Solihull: Helion & Company. Ltd, 2011.

Shakespear, Lt. Col. J, *Historical Records of the 18th (Service) Battalion Northumberland Fusiliers,* Private Distribution, 1920.

Sheldon, Jack, *The German Army on the Somme 1914–1916,* Barnsley: Pen & Sword, 2005.

Sibley, WA, *Wycliffe & The War – A School Record,* Gloucester: John Bellows, 1923.

Stacke, Capt. HF, MC, *The Worcestershire Regiment In The Great War,* Uckfield: The Naval & Military Press Ltd, reprint, 2002.

Stedman, Michael, *La Boisselle, Ovillers, Contalmaison,* Barnsley: Leo Cooper, 1997.

Stock Exchange, The, *The Stock Exchange Memorial of Those Who Fell in the Great War 1914–1918,* Uckfield: The Naval & Military Press Ltd, reprint 2001.

Thomas, Hugh, *The Story of Sandhurst,* London: Hutchinson, 1961.

Tonbridge School, *Tonbridge School & the Great War of 1914–1919,* Uckfield: The Naval & Military Press Ltd, reprint 2006.

Various, *Deeds That Thrilled The Empire,* Uckfield: The Naval & Military Press Ltd, reprint 2002.

Whitehead, Ralph, *The Other Side Of The Wire Vol. I,* Solihull: Helion & Company. Ltd, 2010.

—— *The Other Side Of The Wire Vol. II,* Solihull: Helion & Company. Ltd, 2013.

Wylly, Col. HC, *1st & 2nd Battalions The Sherwood Foresters In The Great War,* Uckfield: The Naval & Military Press Ltd, reprint 2004.

Wyrall, Everard, *The Nineteenth Division 1914–1918,* Uckfield: The Naval & Military Press Ltd, reprint 2009.

Index

INDEX OF PEOPLE

INDEX OF PLACES

INDEX OF MILITARY UNITS & FORMATIONS

INDEX OF GENERAL & MISCELLANEOUS TERMS